Endorsements:

"Substantive help for adoptive mothers is such a neglected topic in our culture. In this book Linda Rice has thoughtfully addressed the unique challenges of feeling an emotional distance, anger from the adoptive child, discouragement, regrets, and much more that an adoptive mother will often experience. If you desire to address these in a biblically helpful way, this book will be your main resource and welcomed help. I believe this book will address most of the difficulties you face as a non-biological mother. It will also be a wonderful resource for biblical counselors seeking to help adoptive mothers with real Scriptural counsel. This book has my strong endorsement!"

— **Dr. John D. Street**, Chair, Graduate Department in Biblical Counseling; President, Association of Certified Biblical Counselors (ACBC) Board of Trustees

---

"*Strengthening the Adoptive Mom* will benefit mothers who find themselves in this particular season of life. Rice's work abounds with Scripture, provides ample application points, and unhesitatingly directs believers back to the gospel of Jesus Christ. Not only will this book give guidance in difficulties and scenarios with adopted children, this book also biblically navigates the issues of biblical parenting in general. All parents will find this work to be helpful in remembering the character of God, the glory of grace, the power of the Spirit, the duty to obey, and the primacy of God's glory. Read this much-needed book and be blessed by its robust biblical arguments and relevant application points."

— **Geoffrey R. Kirkland**, Pastor, Christ Fellowship Bible Church

---

"God comforts us by drawing our attention to Him. 'Eyes on me,' He says. Linda helps adoptive families do just that. By drawing our attention and affections to God through His Word, Linda provides outstanding encouragement and strength to adoptive parents in order for them to love their child best. This is a wonderful resource for adoptive families and I pray God will use this book to glorify Himself for years to come."

— **Dr. Andrew D. Rogers**, author of *Counseling Adoptive Families: The Glorious Truths of the Doctrine of Adoption*, Executive Director of Overseas Instruction in Counseling, Ministry Development Pastor at Kindred Community Church in Anaheim Hills, California

"Adoption is a good thing, but not every good thing is easy. Many adoptive families, mothers in particular, find that our kind intentions toward our child(ren) are often met with indifference, resistance, alienation, hostility, and even violence. If you find yourself living somewhere along this spectrum with your child(ren), whether adopted, foster, or biological, you will find compassion, clarity, comfort, and hope as you read Linda's insightful counsel. My sincere prayer is that you will find Linda's commitment to counseling God's Word with care and conviction a kind and gracious provision of the Lord to you as it was to me personally in the aftermath of adoption-related trials."

— **Connie Dugas**, adoptive mother, pastor's wife, biblical counselor

---

"Linda provides both wise counsel and gracious instruction through the lens of scripture with these meditations. She draws us into the practical sense of what it means to take Christ at His Word and respond in humble obedience. As an adoptive mom dealing with turbulent trials in my own home, I have needed both encouragement and godly instruction from other women in the faith. In a sense, these meditations represent the older woman instructing the younger to love our husbands and children, aiming our hearts in faith to serve and glorify Christ our Lord."

— **Kristin**, adoptive mother, Texas

"This uplifting resource offers much needed encouragement for adoptive moms. I highly recommend you turn to it for help in an often lonely and misunderstood parenting journey."

— **Julie**, adoptive mother, Illinois

"Linda Rice is a wise counselor on an uncomfortable subject. She has not only opened the door for discussion on things painful and unpleasant, but has brought much needed help using the Scriptures as her source and guide. By God's grace her first book, *Parenting the Difficult Child*, has helped many, including me. My prayer is this book would help many more."

— **Dinah**, adoptive mother, Georgia

Strengthening the Adoptive Mom

Hope and Help for Adoptive and Foster Moms

Strengthening the Adoptive Mom

Hope and Help for Adoptive and Foster Moms

Linda J. Rice

—SeedSown Press—

Published by: SeedSown Press

Printed in the United States of America

978-0-9850431-6-2

Book design by Bennett Book Design, St. Louis, Missouri
www.bennettbookdesign.com

*To my sweet mother, Aleen Mittelberg, who provided a wonderful
role model of wise, firm, and gentle, self-sacrificing love for her children.*

*To all the mothers who give of themselves to adopt, foster, or
otherwise help children in need.*

Table of Contents

Acknowledgments

DISCUSSIONS WITH FIVE precious adoptive moms motivated me to write this book. I am grateful to Julie, Connie, Erin, Kristin, and Dinah for entrusting me with their trials and griefs while simultaneously exemplifying biblical parenting wisdom and Christlike love for children who reject them. Their influence sharpened the practicality of the chapters ahead.

Specifically, I thank Connie Dugas, adoptive mom, friend and fellow biblical counselor. Although she and I were both thinking about a book like this, I might not have written it if she hadn't mentioned it. She brainstormed with me, provided helpful insights, and reviewed it. Thank you, Connie, for graciously bumping me into the race I should already have been running and cheering me on as I ran.

Training in biblical counseling revolutionized my life and gently turned me to the service of counseling I had previously decided to avoid. I am thankful for John Street, Stuart Scott, Jay Adams, Wayne Mack, Ernie Baker, The Master's University (California), and the Association of Certified Biblical Counselors. Their training equipped me.

For the two years on this project, Mike, my dear husband, has listened, advised, and urged me forward. He consistently encourages me to both counsel and write. I am grateful for his faithful love of our children and his self-sacrifice for the welfare of others.

Most of all, I thank the Lord Jesus Christ for His great grace for parenting and for the writing of this book.

Introduction

AFTER MORE THAN two years of paperwork and waiting, we were finally on our second trip to Honduras to finalize the adoptions of two children to add to our biological four-year-old waiting at home. Excited and tense, we attended more meetings, paid more fees, and completed more paperwork. Finally, after a long flight, we arrived home exhausted with two precious, frightened, distrustful preschoolers. Would they bond with us? Could we teach them wisdom and influence them to love Christ? Would our hope of a happy family be fulfilled? What had we gotten ourselves into?

Parenting reaps some of the greatest rewards in life. There are many delights, much laughter, discoveries, adventures, achievements, and the joy of serving the Lord by serving your family.

At the same time, parenting is a challenge. This is true for every child, whether biological, adopted, or fostered, whether handicapped or healthy. Parenting reveals our weaknesses, bringing about challenges that become opportunities to trust God, see His faithful work, build godliness, and grow in grace and love for God.

The extra challenges presented by adoptive parenting provoked me to rethink concepts learned from a college psychology course and popular Christian self-help books, such as beliefs about needs, self-esteem, child bonding, and disorders. Difficulties motivated me to study the Word of God for what God says about children, needs, self-esteem, suffering, trauma, and parenting. This eventually led to my first book, *Parenting the Difficult Child: A Biblical Perspective of Reactive Attachment Disorder.*

Other adoptive moms have told me of challenges similar to mine. I so appreciate their unwavering commitment to love their children and be faithful to God in their parenting. It is discussions with them and the urging of Connie Dugas, a pastor's wife, adoptive mom, biblical counselor, and friend, which moved me to write this meditational.[1]

Intended Audience

I hope that your adopted (or foster) child brings you much joy. Maybe, though, you have a child who is trending toward waywardness. Does it seem that managing a challenging child has taken over your life? Do

---

1. A devotional is laser-focused on promoting the reader's devotion to God. While I hope this book promotes your devotion to God, the focus of these meditations is a mixture of devotion to God and relationship with man. Therefore, I am calling it a meditational.

you need perspective? Sensing emotional distance between you and him despite your every effort to bond, are you feeling apprehensive? Does your child seem inordinately angry? Are you? Does it seem that parents of biological children don't understand, so you feel isolated? Perhaps you find yourself in spiritual battles against disillusionment, frustration, regrets, or despair.

This book is also for counselors of adoptive or foster mothers. Meditations can be assigned as appropriate.

Purpose of the Book

There are already many resources encouraging pre- and early-adoptive parents. While I hope this book contributes to that category, what I have set for our focus is the adoptive or foster mom of a child who is persisting in behaviors difficult to handle—a child who seems to reject his family. This book is not intended to be a parenting-methods manual, so much as a supplement to encourage mothers in the worldview that undergirds godly, biblical parenting. So while I'll address some issues of the child, the focus is on strengthening moms so that they can better help their children while keeping their hearts and minds aimed on Christ and His Word. This book does not propose to be comprehensive, but it does spotlight some truths vital for mothers of all kinds of children, especially the troubled and resistant.

The Bible is the best resource for parents because, in His Word, God speaks to all of our concerns. Scripture teaches, answers questions, and corrects our thinking, which wonderfully strengthens the heart and guides our actions. The Bible reveals God and shows how He Himself is the ultimate solution to all our problems.

I hope you will perceive understanding and compassion for the weakness or grief a parent might feel, but I'm not going to stay there. Do parents get hurt? Yes, but we set ourselves aside and do what is in the best interest of the child and God's glory. If you are a child of God, you are commissioned by the King of the universe to parent His way with love, gentleness, confidence, boldness, and strength.

Adoption is a wonderful institution. Yet, it can be a rough go. As Connie says, "Adoption is good. It can be very hard. Hard is not bad." Adoption is not for everyone, but can be tremendously rewarding. Whether your children are in the home or grown-and-flown, whether your relationship is sailing smoothly or has hit rough waters, this book can help you gain perspective that will strengthen you for the long haul.

Organization of the Book

To help personalize the book, I would like you to meet the fictionalized couple Bert and Bessie, adoptive parents of Donnie, to whom I refer in several meditations. I chose the names figuring that few people nowadays use them. They represent a wide range of adoptive couples who observe in their children bizarre behaviors common, though not universal, to adopted children. They are Christians. They may be the couple who adopted a child through foster care, an infant from China, a toddler from India, older sisters from Russia, a family of five from Latin America.

They may have adopted because they thought it was the Christian thing to do—they were told that adoption is what God does and that to care for the orphans Christians "should" adopt. Or, they may have adopted because they struggled to conceive biological children of their own. Or perhaps they adopted because adoptive families fascinate them, or because they just plain wanted more children to love.

I have personally grappled with every concept in this book, but no situation of Bessie is unique to me and Bessie; I shaped her situations by a variety of cases I have heard.

The meditations are grouped by topic, starting with foundational concepts such as a biblical view of family and the institution of adoption. Then the book zooms in to take a closer look at the child and parenting perspectives. Next are meditations on the turbulent emotions and attitudes a parent might experience. The final meditations are intended to set your feet for endurance that pleases God. However, after reading the first meditation, the rest can be read in any order.

Some concepts are repeated. This is no mistake. Parenting oppositional children can sorely try a parent. Seeing the same truth from different verses and angles can develop a needed concept and reinforce it in the mind.

What I Hope to Accomplish

This book is a tool you might use to bring the Bible to bear upon the difficulties you face in parenting. I hope it motivates you to go to the scripture of the day and read the verses before and after. Seeing the passage in context will broaden your understanding and impress it more indelibly on your mind. Scripture, applied by the Holy Spirit, is what restores the soul, makes wise, and rejoices the heart (Psalm 19:7-8).

I hope that this book will help equip you for the welfare of your children. The more you grow in godliness, the more blessed they will be, and the better able you will be to build relationship.

What I most hope to accomplish is to strengthen you for parenting to the glory of God and the deepening of your relationship with Him. You can't truly grasp His love for you unless you have a right view of God, a right view of self, and a right view of the child, which all come from Scripture. You need to take on God's goals and handle emotions His way. And you need hope. God's Word applied by the Holy Spirit provides hope and strength that will enable you to overcome temptations. That enablement is God's grace at work in you for the glory of Christ. May you have joy as you see Him work in you and your family. To God be the glory!

Strengthening the Adoptive Mom

Hope and Help for Adoptive and Foster Moms

The Word of God Is Abundantly Sufficient

*All Scripture is God-breathed and profitable for teaching, for reproof,
for correction, for training in righteousness, so that the man of God may
be equipped, having been thoroughly equipped for every good work.*

~ 2 Timothy 3:16-17, LSB

BERT AND BESSIE have found several organizations that offer help for parenting adopted children who present with difficulty. The suggested theories and methods make sense and seem to work, so they change their parenting practices as advised. This approach is pragmatic, but is it biblical? Whose counsel is true and authoritative?

In 2 Timothy 3, Paul says that the Word of God is able to teach the truth about how to live, provide reproof when we sin, alert us to mistakes, correct us back onto the path of obedience, and train us to stay on the path. Is any phase of growing wise in parenting left out of that cycle? The Word applied in the power of the Spirit enables believers to do *"every* good work." Is any word or action excluded from "every good work"?

Paul was addressing the fact that cultural ideologies were influencing Timothy and the church—including views of psychology. This is still true. Paul reassures Timothy that the Word of God is sufficient, effectual, and authoritative, as no psychology can be. The age of brain imaging is not the only generation to be able to solve emotional/behavioral problems. For example, if God, who knows all things, knew that jumping jacks or sitting a certain way is a parenting method essential to dealing with an unruly child, He would have written so. If we need attachment theory, or if a child can't be saved or live obediently to God without changing neural pathways, God would have told us. In the Word of God, our Father has given all that is essential for life and godliness, including parental wisdom (2 Peter 1:3).

Scripture tells how to love, how to treat authorities, and how to handle offenses, trauma, suffering, and a difficult past—all issues of troubled children. It teaches how to handle emotions, including fear, anger, anxiety, sadness, and despair. It contains all necessary principles of child development, conscience, bonding, alienation, identity, communication, and parenting. It explains why people do what they do and how to change habits of thought and behavior. It defines what change looks like and produces salvation and sanctification for Christlikeness.

In the Bible, God covered everything parents need for helping adopted children. No other source of counsel can legitimately make such a claim.

Many Christians think they can integrate man's "truth" with God's for a better result. But even if behavior improves, man's ways fall far short of the gospel and of the pursuit of sanctification for the glory of God.

Not just any parenting method is acceptable to God. Jesus didn't resort to man's methods. In Mark 10:17-27, the rich young ruler came asking, "How do I gain eternal life?" (Isn't that what we want our kids to ask?) Jesus told him a certain biblical means. The ruler refused and walked away without satisfaction and without God. Jesus didn't resort to psychology to persuade him; He stated the truth graciously and trusted God with the ruler's reaction. That is what parents must do. With love, teach the truth from the Word of God. With compassion, discipline disobedience according to the Word of God. Trust God throughout, even when the child doesn't respond wisely.

The Word of God through the gospel of Jesus Christ practiced by the power of the Spirit is authoritative, abundantly sufficient, and powerfully effectual.

Reflection
- Why are not all methodologies acceptable as long as they work? (Hint: While all truth is God's truth, all lies are the devil's lies. We are more deceivable than we think. And define "work.")
- Do the parenting resources you read and consult lead you first to Scripture?

Implementation
- When you have a parenting question, seek your answer first from the Bible. Use resources that show you the answers in Scripture.
- From the list of issues above, choose one (fear, anger, sadness, child development, conscience, identity, communication, etc.). Study scripture on it and plan how to use what you learn with your child.

Blessings of Adoption

Adoption by God Is a Privilege

*… that He might redeem those who were under the Law, that we might
receive the adoption as sons. Because you are sons, God has sent the Spirit
of His Son into our hearts, crying out, "Abba! Father!" Therefore you are
no longer a slave, but a son; and if a son, then an heir through God.*

~ Galatians 4:5-7

THE ONLY ADOPTION most Christians will experience is their adoption into
God's family. As emphasized in Galatians 4, it is a place of relational intimacy and connection by permanent membership in a new family under the
care and control of the new Father. For the Christian, this happens when the
Son has redeemed, the Spirit has regenerated to make the redeemed person
new, and the Father has adopted that new person into His family—all by
grace and done in love. The convicted slave is moved from the courtroom
to the home. The Judge drops His judicial robes and becomes the Father.

By adoption, the Father heaps a multitude of blessings on his child.
The Christian,

- is no longer in the previous family and way of living,
- is no longer under the law,
- is placed as a son in God's family, made not a cousin or a grandchild,
  but a son,
- is now tied to the new family culture that leads to life and joy,
- has a Father committed to providing, protecting, and nurturing,
  who takes special, personal interest in his welfare,
- has clothing given by the new Father—the robe of Christ's righteousness,
- has spiritual food,
- is in an intimate relationship with a Father who began loving sacrifi-
  cially long before the adoption (God talks to him–by His Word–and
  listens to him–in his prayers.),
- has the right to call this one "dearest Father,"
- has legal right to appeal to God for help and privileges in a way that
  no non-family child may do,
- receives chastisement intended for protection and instruction and
  restoration of relationship,
- has a special Comforter given by the Father,
- has siblings, united with others who share the same father and family
  values,

- has equal rights and privileges with all the children in God's family,
- is identified by the family name,
- has a special book written about his Father and family history, explaining the Father's intents and instructing how to have the most abundant enjoyment in God's family,
- shares in the riches of God's family–love, traditions, provisions, daily communion, family experiences, and inheritance.

Adoption by God is one of the greatest privileges of a Christian. It is a supreme blessing to the believer and we rightly rejoice in it. However, adoption is not primarily for our blessing but for God's glory. As His grateful children, His glory should be our greatest reason for joy.

Have you been adopted by God? Only those He saves are adopted. You must recognize that you have sinned and, by Law, the wage earned is hell, so you need saving. Jesus, the Son of God, died on the cross to "redeem," to pay the wage for sin. Repent from your way of meriting God's acceptance. Trust only in Christ for salvation.

Reflection

- How can a person be adopted by God? How is the gospel related?
- In what ways is adoption a blessing to the believer? How does that inspire your love for God?
- Human adoption incorporates many of these same types of blessings. What about your adoption by God might be helpful for your child to hear to show him the hope of the gospel?

Implementation

- Have you repented from your sins to believe in Christ alone for your salvation? Read Romans 3:23; 6:23; 5:8; 10:9-10; and Ephesians 2:1-9. Write a paragraph stating what these passages say about how to be saved from the penalty of sin and stand in right relation to God.
- From what in your past are you redeemed and freed?
- How might having God as Father rather than as Judge affect your approach to Him?
- Spend time five mornings or evenings this week using the blessings listed above in thanks to God.

MEDITATION 3:

Adoption of Children Is a Privilege

*He predestined us to adoption as sons through Jesus Christ to Himself,
according to the kind intention of His will, to the praise of the glory of
His grace, which He freely bestowed on us in the Beloved.*

~ Ephesians 1:5, NASB

CENTURIES AGO, WITH "kind intention," the Son of God traveled from the pure, glorious culture of heaven to the sinful, decaying culture on earth to make it possible for His Father to adopt children. Here's how: Even though sinners belong to Satan's family and are enemies of God, it pleased Jesus to come, welcome, serve, and suffer for them. Ultimately, He paid the supreme price of redemption–His life.

Because of Christ's payment, the Spirit can regenerate the redeemed through a new birth, giving them a new heart. Then, in adoption, all legal ties to the previous family are severed, including all obligations. The Father, by adoption, legally grants those former enemies permanent family membership with all the rights and privileges of a son. They have a new identity. This was God's choice, motivated by love, all for the praise of His glory.

God adopts because He takes pleasure in doing so. He wants these children. Believers can't earn it and don't bring any inherent benefit with them into the family. Also, they can't sabotage it and the Father won't annul the adoption. As an adoptive Father, what does God gain? Besides a lot of trouble from immature or uncooperative children, here are a few delights for Him:

- children He considers precious,
- the joy of loving them,
- enjoyment of relationships,
- a growing family of worshipers,
- a bride to give to His Son,
- the joy of transforming a sinner into the image of His own pure Son,
- more image-bearers walking around earth shining His glory wherever they go,
- greater glory to Himself.

With sacrifices, sorrows, and joys, adoptive parents get to experience in human adoption a small sampling of what the Father does in spiritual adoption. Their loving sacrifices begin long before meeting the child. They legally grant their name and equal status with other children by the family name. Pouring themselves into the child's life, they provide food and clothing, affection and protection, prayers, thought, planning, play, evangelism, instruction, and discipline. They sacrifice for the child's welfare and seek the child's growth and blessing. They also receive the pleasure of knowing precious children, of fun in play, of watching them discover and grow, of relationships. Adoptive parents desire the joys of loving, of relating, and of participating with God to hopefully shape a little person into a lover of God.

Reflection

- Do you view your adopted child as a "ministry" or as a family member? How does that compare with how you view a biological child? How does God view His children?
- Is your adoptive child resisting a trustful relationship with you? How might you use God's kind adoption of you to motivate you to greater love toward your adopted child?

Implementation

- Thank God for adopting you when you deserved the opposite.
- Thank God for the privilege of experiencing a taste of what it is like for Him to adopt imperfect children.
- Recall times you have rejected the counsel and/or discipline of your heavenly Father and thank Him for His forbearance and forgiveness.

*A Biblical View
of the Family*

MEDITATION 4:

Marriage Takes Priority

Therefore a man shall leave his father and his mother, and cleave to his wife; and they shall become one flesh.

~ Genesis 2:24

IT IS NO secret that raising children requires devotion and copious amounts of time. Unintentionally, parents may gradually neglect each other as they increasingly focus on the children. After all, a mom's priority should be her children, right?

Actually, Genesis teaches that marriage is the higher priority. It explains that after God made everything else, He formed the first man with special care. From the man, He took a rib and constructed a woman; she was handcrafted to be the perfect complement to Adam and the most fitting companion. Then God "brought her to the man," a gift from God to man. Thus began the first marriage.

Notice, there is not a child in sight. Adam and Eve were the first family. Later, Cain was born to them and when he grew up, just as Genesis 2:24 says, he left and joined his wife, forming another family. And so it went with family after family to this day.

Marriage is not a social construct; it was established by God—it was His idea. He intended that "a man shall leave his father and his mother and be joined to his wife, and they shall become one flesh"—a new family (Genesis 2:24, NIV). The word "joined" infers a permanent union. "One flesh" refers to complete unity in all aspects of living, not just physically. A child is a result of that union, but does not become a partner in it. Children come and go; spouses remain.

The New Testament reiterates this priority. In Ephesians 5-6, Colossians 3, and 1 Peter 3, God speaks to husbands and wives before speaking to parents and children. Therefore, the priority relationship for husband and wife must be the marriage.

Children certainly need care, care that absorbs time, energy, emotions, and sleep like a paper towel absorbs water. Adopted children often need more care, at least for a time. The raising of children places numerous stressors on the marriage relationship; a difficult child multiplies them.

Stressors may include a lack of time alone for talk and intimacy. One parent or the other may feel discouraged by a child's prolonged misbehavior, a barrage of manipulations, and lack of salvation. While important, these must not be allowed to supersede the priority of the marriage.

If the marriage is in trouble, parenting concerns will multiply. Keep the marriage healthy and, even if the children choose waywardness, spouses will work as a team and glorify God by prioritizing one another as their primary ministry responsibility.

Reflection

- How might prioritizing your marriage affect your reactions when your children want your attention while you are talking with your husband?
- In what ways do you prioritize your spouse over your children?
- What can parents do to raise children to leave the home and not stay?

Implementation

- Make time for your spouse. Plan time together sans children. Talk about non-family topics. Do something you both enjoy. Plan time regularly and guard that time diligently.
- When children are present, prioritize your spouse. Don't interrupt listening to him/her when your child comes, wanting your attention.
- If you have a particularly difficult, emotionally-draining child, plan times of respite away from children. If you seek respite only when a crisis hits, the child will feel rejected. If you have pre-planned times, the child may not welcome it, but won't be as inclined to view it as punishment.

Pursue Unity in Your Marriage

*For this reason, a man shall leave his father and mother and be joined
to his wife, and the two shall become one flesh. This is a profound
mystery–but I am talking about Christ and the church.*

~ Ephesians 5:31-32, NIV

MARRIAGE IS ABOUT so much more than two people's happiness. Marriage reflects the glorious union between Christ and His church. "In Christ" (Ephesians 1:1-14), Christians are one new humanity (ch. 2-3), and the church is Christ's one body (ch. 4), walking united in the Spirit (ch. 5-6). Reflecting this, marriage has epochal impact. It is one means for God to work out His unfolding plan of redemption for kingdom rule to His glory.

As the church is one with Christ, so married couples are to be one, united in spiritual matters, sharing of thoughts, finances, and social life. It means agreement on goals and parenting practices. The degree of unity or disunity will affect everything in the home.

Divide and conquer is a common tactic children employ. With adopted children, the mom is usually the one viewed as an enemy. Since Dad receives the charm, he finds it hard to believe Mom's descriptions of little Donnie's oppositional behaviors. Conflict ensues.

Being able to play one parent against the other provokes loss of respect for both and undermines the parents' authority. Division stirs confusion and insecurity in children. Worse, division does not model the unity of Christ and His church.

Unity has a calming effect. United authorities restore order, enforce justice, and protect the innocent. Reinforced by Dad, Mom has more power for maintaining order. Parental unity is a fire retardant to a household otherwise inflamed in conflict. Parents at peace with one another are safer to approach with a concern or appeal. Most importantly, unity pleases God because it displays the unity of Christ and His church.

Parents are not primarily a dad and mom. They are first and foremost a husband and wife. In the presence of the children, both spouses must take the same stand, discussing disagreements privately. They need to work toward having the same mind (Ephesians 4:1-3).

Generally speaking, more detriments result from disunity of parents than from mistakes in parenting. The benefit of one parent's wiser decision will be nullified by disunity. Better they together make a wrong choice for the child than to sacrifice marital unity.

Reflection

- What does Ephesians say about how your marriage is bigger than you? How does it affect your family? Church? Neighbors? Missions? The reputation and purposes of God?
- How does God's bigger purpose for marriage inspire your awe of God?
- Your husband will make mistakes. What can you do to promote unity in the difficult times?
- How can you think and act toward your husband like the church is to Christ?

Implementation

- Read all of Ephesians and record how marriage relates to each section. Why did Paul write about marriage in this book of theology? In what ways is marriage about much more than you and your husband? How does this truth affect the value you place on marital unity?
- After separations, like coming home from work, greet each other before greeting the kids.
- Learn and practice godly communication for solving problems and reconciling relationships.
- If/when your child attempts to play one parent against the other, ask, "What did your dad/mom say?"

God Composed Your Family

For You formed my inward parts;
You wove me in my mother's womb.
I will give thanks to You, for I am fearfully and wonderfully made;
Wonderful are Your works,
And my soul knows it very well.
My frame was not hidden from You,
When I was made in secret,
And skillfully wrought in the depths of the earth;
Your eyes have seen my unformed substance;
And in Your book all of them were written
The days that were formed for me,
When as yet there was not one of them.

~ Psalm 139:13-16

THEY SAY GROWING old isn't for sissies. Neither is parenting. What an immense responsibility to shape another person's character and know it is likely to influence him for the rest of his life. Mix in an extra challenging child. Complicate it with your weaknesses, mistakes, failures, and outright sins. Some days as a parent are overwhelming.

The sovereignty of God becomes a tremendously comforting doctrine. Since all our days are ordained, then God must be in control of events in each day. Since God controls all things, you can know with certainty that it is God who placed your child into your home. Yes, you made choices, but however you planned, God directs your steps (Proverbs 16:9). Had it not been His will you would have been unable to adopt this child.

Having woven the child in utero, He designed your child's DNA and the resulting characteristics, talents, and weaknesses. He ordained your adopted child's past, including any losses, accidents, and even maltreatment, all for some good purpose. God knows how your child's past has influenced him, whether toward wisdom or alienation, fear, and anger. God knows when your child sits and stands, knows his thoughts before the words cross his lips (Psalm 139:1-4). The challenges your child faces are not thwarting the plan of God; they are incorporated miraculously into that plan as providence.

For some reason, and it is a good reason, God gave you the stewardship of this particular child. He placed your child with you knowing the influences your strengths and weaknesses would have. He knew that you would not always respond biblically and that some of your mistakes would exacerbate your child's sinful propensities. He knew when and how you would both succeed and fail to parent the way He directs.

The child in your family is not a mistake and not a quirk of chance. God intentionally superintended the placement of that child with you. You can trust God that the composition of your family is His will for you at this time. The challenges you face as a parent are not obstacles; they are opportunities—opportunities to respond accordingly, opportunities to grow in faith and character, and opportunities to believe God is sovereign, good, and powerful to turn all to the good for His glory.

Reflection

- ❧ What is the significance of the doctrine of sovereign providence for your situation?
- ❧ How does submitting to the wise and loving sovereignty of God help you be content with the family you have, with all its quirks and troubles?

Implementation

- ❧ Take a few minutes to pray through Psalm 139 with praise to God concerning the difficult people in your family.
- ❧ Knowing that God has placed this child under your influence for His good purpose, do the next parenting responsibility boldly.
- ❧ When you fail, repent and then move forward again, trusting that the sovereign God has chosen to work His plan providentially through you and your child, however difficult that may be.

A Biblical View
of the Adopted Child

Maltreatment Leaves a Mark

*She said to them, "Do not call me Naomi; call me Mara, for the
Almighty has dealt very bitterly with me."*

~ Ruth 1:20

MY FRIEND JAN was walking her son's Boston terrier, Tillman. When two
baby kittens came to greet him, he, a grown dog, squealed in fear and
tried to jump in her arms. Why such an unreasonable reaction? Years
earlier, when Tillman was a curious pup, he was smacked in the nose by
a cat. Pain left a lasting mark.[1]

The same happens with people.[2] Consider Naomi, whose name
means "pleasant." She had a pleasing personality and a knowledge of the
Word of God. When a famine struck, her husband led his family to a
foreign land, then died, "and she was left with her two sons" (Ruth 1:3).
Both sons married foreign women, then died, so she was destitute. One
daughter-in-law, Ruth, stayed with Naomi and helped her return to her
homeland. There, she told her friends to call her Mara, "bitter," "for the
Almighty has dealt very bitterly with me." Amidst severe losses, Naomi
had twisted from pleasant to bitter.

Then through Ruth's companionship and marriage, her circumstances shifted into happier times. Even so, when Ruth gave Naomi a
grandson, it was the town women, not Naomi, who identified him as
Naomi's redemption (4:14-15). The effects of hardships were still present.
Agonies had marked her.

Children are wired to interpret their experiences. Their interpreta-
tions result in emotional responses and shape a sense of identity.

Adopted children undergo emotionally painful experiences. Infants
lose a familiar mom. Many children have received neglect and abuse. Being
suddenly immersed in an unfamiliar family culture under the control of
strangers is an additional shock. Children are not as equipped as adults to
understand and rightly respond to severe trials. They don't have the adult
capacity for logic, the history of life experiences, or a sound theology to

---

1. A true story from Jan, a friend, North Carolina
2. This idea as a biblical concept was introduced to me by John Street in three lectures on Psalm 55
which he delivered at Grace Community Church. "The Imprecatory Psalms," 11/17/2006, 12/31/2006,
2/4/2007. https://www.gracechurch.org/sermons/language/0?page=24&searchteacher=john%20
street&books=0&chapters=0&verses=0&searchType=0

counter false perceptions and find solutions. Loss, betrayal, neglect, abandonment, and abuse can sear like a branding iron. They mark a child.

While Ruth provided compassionate gentleness and opportunities for Naomi to step into normal mother-in-law responsibilities (Ruth 2:19-22; 3:1-4, 16-18; 4:16), Naomi's friends may have been put off or confused by her reaction. Sure, she had had a hard time, but, "You're back home now." Did they understand? We hope some did.

As with Naomi's friends, adoptive parents may not know the child's past trials or realize how extensive the effects of maltreatment can be. All they see is the present habituated reaction, like Tillman's automatic attempt to climb Jan like a tree. Don't call me pleasant, call me bitter.

Depending on the degree of maltreatment and the particular child's resilience, the effects of past traumatic hardship may exert more or less continued influence. Some will practice destructive thinking. Others will choose right responses until the marking fades into an ever-more-distant past. Adoptive parents can be a significant influence toward the latter by guiding the child's heart to Christ.

Reflection

- What have you done to overcome the effects of a hurtful event in your past? How much effort has it required?
- Discuss with your spouse how the following might be true of your child: Anger can feel like a safer emotion than fear because it provides a mirage of control and power; it hides fear. How might a gentle tone assuage anger?
- How would it affect your approach if you assume your child is resilient and not a victim?

Implementation

- List behaviors of your child which might result from habituated fear and self-preservation.
- List truths about God that would have given Naomi a correct perspective. Plan how to teach one to your child.
- What can you do to demonstrate compassion and gentleness in light of your child's painful past while moving the child forward in present responsibilities?

Betrayal Breaks Trust

> *Do not devise harm against your neighbor,*
> *While he lives securely beside you.*
> *Do not contend with a man without cause,*
> *If he has dealt you no harm.*
>
> ~ Proverbs 3:29-30

FAMILY IS THERE for you, right? The family was certainly *there* for Joseph. Joseph was number eleven of twelve sons. Think of that—ten older brothers to help and defend you! When, at his dad's request, the teen-aged Joseph traveled far from home to check on his brothers who were herding sheep, they turned on him. Now imagine *that*—ten grown men grab you and throw you into a well. You overhear them plotting to kill you. Then, they sell you to a passing slave trader who drags you away from all you've known. Your own brothers! Those who should protect instead betray (Genesis 37).

Children are wired to trust because trust is a vital element of worship and all humans are made to worship. So all are wired to trust someone or something.[1]

It is, therefore, natural to trust those who live with you in your house. We know them the most intimately and depend upon them every day for companionship, protection, and provisions. There is no neighbor closer than one who lives with you, so you are more vulnerable emotionally and physically to family than to anyone outside. Therefore, betrayal by family is also the most painful of betrayals.

By the very nature of adoption, the child, to one degree or another, has felt a sense of loss or even harm. In infant adoption, the newborn's mother is suddenly not there; the voices he hears and the touch he feels are unfamiliar and uncomfortable (even if helpful), which likely stirs uncertainty. Perhaps an older pre-adoptive infant is left for hours, crying for food. Maybe the young child felt the lash of cruel words or physical pain. If the caregiver doesn't take the time to teach otherwise, he is in frequent uncertainty about the wisest behavior in various situations. If a

---

1. Attachment theory proposes that ability and propensity to trust are attributes developed through evolution for survival. This belief totally disregards God. It shifts perspective from personal responsibility to neediness. The purpose of mankind becomes perpetuation of species rather than worship of God.

caregiver who should provide safety is not trustworthy, a helpless child will naturally feel insecure. If his own family betrays him, who else can he trust?

Then, in adoption, he is forced to live in unfamiliar surroundings with unfamiliar people who have power to hurt him in a multitude of ways. From his perspective, why should he trust or risk feeling affection toward anyone?

We may not know the particular offense that drives an adopted child to slam the door on relationships, but we can understand that experiences have given him some reason to be slow to trust anyone but himself, never realizing that his own heart is not trustworthy (Jeremiah 17:9). Parents need to consistently respond with compassion, respect, understanding, gentleness, and truth. Parents must be trustworthy even if the child chooses to not trust them.

Reflection

- Has anyone ever let you down or even betrayed you? How did you feel? How did your thinking change?
- Christ was attractive to the oppressed. What did He do that inspired a sense of safety with Him?
- How has Jesus' response to the oppressed inspired you to trust Christ?
- Considering your child's past, why might it be unsurprising if he interprets parental denials of his wants, gentle corrections, and godly discipline as painful betrayals?

Implementation

- Are you making sure you do not "contend … without cause" by raising unnecessary conflict (Proverbs 3:30)? How so?
- In what ways are you protecting your child by faithfully limiting and disciplining him even if he interprets it as enmity?
- How might you be more like Christ in tenderness and gentleness toward your child?

MEDITATION 9:

Persevere with the Distrustful

*A brother offended is harder to win over than a strong city
And contentions are like the bars of a citadel.*

~ Proverbs 18:19

IN ANCIENT TIMES cities lay within walls for protection. The most effective walls were thick, high, and deep, with slopes to deflect battering rams. Gates were barred or metal-clad wood. Towers on either side enabled defenders to shoot arrows at attackers from protected perches.[1] This depicts one whose trust has been betrayed.

Children are wired to connect because God made man to be in loving relationship with Him.[2] Yet, many adoptive children come encased in their own walled fortress. They persistently and vigorously refuse to trust their parents. They can remain hypervigilant, secretive, oppositional, and manipulative—generally living as if they were trying to survive among enemies. Proverbs 18:19 provides insight into why trusting can be so difficult for adopted children.

Trust is like an open door to the heart. It allows another to enter, look around, and even sit down and sip coffee with your soul. As trust grows stronger, the other person is invited to explore and come to know what is in the rooms of your soul.

Trust is built on a sense of security. The sense of security is built on repeatedly experiencing faithfulness in the other person. Seeing the other as trustworthy, you don't put up guards against emotional or physical pain because you've learned you don't need to. Perceiving yourself accepted and respected despite faults and failings, you consider it safe to be transparent. Such a child can forget himself and jump with abandon into family activities and learn new skills at risk of failures along the way.

When trust has been broken, the sense of safety vanishes. Suspicion, withdrawal, and secrecy replace openness. Warm communion turns to icy separation. In a more severe breach, the door may be slammed, locked, and a "Keep Out" sign posted. Walls go up; windows are barred. Arrows are shot at those who knock. If continued, distrust becomes a

---

1. Judges 16:3; 1 Kings 4:13; Nehemiah 3:3; Isaiah 45:2. Also, Max Schwartz, *Machines, Buildings, Weaponry of Biblical Times* (Old Tappan, New Jersey: Felming H. Revell Company, 1990), 125-129.
2. The characteristic of human connection is not evolutionary, but God-created for a transcendent purpose (relationship with God) (Genesis 2:23-25; 3:8).

habit and the bars are cemented in place even toward those who have done nothing to cause distrust.

As an adoptive parent, you may find yourself barred outside a citadel. You aren't the brother who did the offending, but the hurt child is hyper-sensitive to his vulnerability under your (rightful) power. The setting of a loving family may feel threatening because it tempts him to trust, which in the past exposed him to painful betrayal. So he fights it.

It is true that a child's trust in parents opens the gate to relationships and learning. However, trust is under the control of the child and can't be forced. If the distrustful child's heart hides in a walled city, parental efforts to gain trust may be interpreted as a dangerous siege. Arrows rain down. So if gaining trust drives what you do and your child persistently refuses, you are pre-set for disappointment, disillusionment, and discouragement.

Scripture never commands parents to gain a child's trust. It commands faithfulness. Do be trustworthy and winsome in love for the child but, more importantly, persevere in biblical parenting in obedience to God, trusting His love for you. You can't force a child to take down the bars, but you can, by God's grace, live in a way that makes the bars unnecessary and glorify God in the process.

Reflection

- Have you ever barred someone out of your life? How did that affect you?
- You are helplessly under God's control. How well do you trust Him?
- How should Proverbs 18:19 affect the expectations of someone who is not trusted by a person severely hurt in the past?
- Which do you think about more, bonding and winning your child's trust, or how to faithfully parent even if your child never trusts you?

Implementation

- Pray about the following trustworthy obedience. Instead of trying to persuade a child to trust you:
  - Don't set your happiness on winning trust so much as on being trustworthy out of love for Christ.
  - Be consistently kind and gentle. Play with your child. Listen to your child.
  - Keep consequences for infractions reasonable. If you promise a consequence, carry it out.
  - If you sin against your child, ask for forgiveness.

Children Are Choosers

My son, do not forget my teaching,
But let your heart keep my commandments.

~ Proverbs 3:1, NASB

THIS FATHER'S POINT is plain. Remember and obey God's commands. Observe an ancillary factor, the father's assumption that his son can choose to forget or remember, to obey or disobey. This assumption underlies all commands. Children are choosers.

It is common to view children as passive receivers, modeling clay shaped by influential circumstances. Therefore, serious behavioral problems must be because of others or trauma. Wounded, they are "stuck" in unhelpful reactions to past painful experiences.

Parents are told to think of them as good at heart, just wounded. Don't call disobedience sin. Build their self-esteem. Discipline differently because adopted children can't figure out that loving discipline is different from abuse.

Focused on meeting felt needs, such parents underestimate the power of the child's will. The child learns to view his problem as outside himself, what others have done to him, so believes he can't help himself. The child remains enslaved to behaviors that offend God and drive people away.

More critically, classing a child as a victim rather than a sinner short-circuits the gospel. Since he is a "good" person, he is just wounded and needs healing, not a sinner who needs forgiveness.

It is true that children are naive and easily influenced, forming perceptions of past experiences which they then use to inaccurately assess present treatment. However, children are not merely passive receivers. Disobedience demonstrates self-direction. Yes, children can be victimized, but they can also choose how they perceive the maltreatment and can choose actions. They do not have to think and act like victims.

Should parents show compassion to an alienated child who may be reacting to past painful experiences? Absolutely! Awareness of the insecurity and fear underlying anger should guide facial expressions, speech, and discipline. With gentle responses, they can teach the child to cry out to God for help.

Just like the Proverbial father, parents communicate hope by treating the child as a chooser. Children *can* learn a biblical view of the past and suffering. They *are capable* of aligning present perceptions (of offenses) with reality. They *can* learn how to resist old thoughts so as to make right choices in the present. It may be hard, but children *can* choose to honor and obey even if they don't trust. They *can* choose to love others no matter how they feel about themselves. All of these choices provide practice in handling trauma God's way so that they can mature into responsibility and enjoy happiness.

Parents demonstrate Christlike love when they, like the father of Proverbs, instruct about right and wrong and then, with love, enforce application and remembrance. Discipline is God's grace to a child because it helps him choose to overcome foolish ways and desire wisdom (Hebrews 12:5-11). That is grace!

Parent, you, too, are a chooser, with a Father who instructs and disciplines you because He loves you. To obey God, you often must choose to go against your feelings and inclinations.

Your child may have suffered, and that rightly hurts your heart, but he is not a victim. He *can* choose differently and enjoy the reward for doing so. Expecting a child to choose the right thing offers him hope—of escape from enslavement to destructive behavior, of rewards, and of a better life—all things a loving mom wants for her child. Don't let pity keep you from calling him to right choices.

Reflection

- What difference does it make in a person's life choices when he views himself as sick or healthy, mentally disordered or morally sinful, victim or chooser?
- In what ways do you observe your child choosing good and bad behaviors?

Implementation

- What scriptures might a parent use to help a child rethink past painful experiences to gain a biblical perspective (a right view of God, of self, and of circumstances)?
- Love for God is the most powerful motivator of right choices. What verses show why God is beloved? With your child, daily list God's goodnesses that you see.
- Study Romans 12:9-21 and 1 Peter 2:11-12, 20-25; 3:17-18; 4:15-16, 19, dealing with unjust treatment. Teach these passages to your child, especially highlighting the gospel.

God Can Change the Heart of a Child

The king's heart is like channels of water in the hand of Yahweh;
He turns it wherever He pleases.

~ Proverbs 21:1

How DELIGHTFUL IS the child who has a tender heart! He is receptive to instruction and correction, with a conscience increasingly sensitized to the things of God. Godly parents long for this kind of heart in their children because they know God will be glorified and the child will grow in wisdom and, as a result, be blessed abundantly in life.

It grieves parents when a child's heart is resistant. Some are so impervious to appeals that they endure any penalty to outlast any authority, even police and social services. The heart is set in granite. It seems nothing can persuade him to do what is right. Parents are tempted to give up hope.

Proverbs 21:1 says God turns a king's heart wherever He pleases. At the time Proverbs was written, a despotic king was autonomous, accountable to no person or governing body on earth. He could do whatever he wanted in remorseless domination. He need not bend his will to anyone. That much power becomes addictive. Only if another king conquered him could he be subdued or displaced. Think of the pharaohs, Artaxerxes, Alexander the Great, Constantine, Stalin, and Hitler.

God is more powerful; He can bend the will of a despot without violating his will. He just shifts the channel and the king's will follows. For example, Pharaoh declared he would never let the Hebrews go. God persuaded him to not only let them go, but drive them out (Exodus 5:2; 6:1; 12:31). Centuries later, the conquering Sennacherib laid siege to Jerusalem. God arranged events to change his mind so he voluntarily returned home without conquering Jerusalem (1 Kings 18-19). Nebuchadnezzar exulted so much in his autonomy that he declared himself a god. At the height of his power, the true God humbled him until he acknowledged that God, not himself, ruled supremely (Daniel 4). If God can change the heart of a proud, stubborn, ruthless, despot most entrenched in power, He can change the heart of the most hardened person, including a remorseless child.

Consider:
- Dead is dead. The heart of the rebellious is not more dead than that of the compliant.

- The God who resurrects bodies regenerates hearts. What power! Trust Him.
- Only God can regenerate (Ezekiel 36; Titus 3:5). This truth removes the expectation (or right) that what you do has to "work." Rest in Him.
- Just because God hasn't changed a person's heart doesn't mean He can't. This truth removes from you the weight of responsibility when what you do does not work. Trust Him.
- Just because He can doesn't mean He will. Submit to Him.
- Even if He doesn't change the child's heart, He is is still perfectly good. Supremely gracious, God will use all parental actions, even unwise or sinful ones, providentially for His good purposes. Believe Him.

Reflection

- Can a child in rebellion thwart the will of God? Why or why not?
- Can parental mistakes prevent a child from godly responses?
- Why is it most loving for parents to allow and provide consequences? How is it unloving to protect the child from most consequences?
- How can Proverbs 21:1 convey hope to a parent whose child seems persistently committed to waywardness?

Implementation

- Review the "Consider" bullet points in the discussion. List what you can do to practice trusting God with the heart of your child. Do (or stop doing) one action today and tell a trusted person about it.
- What would help you grow more consistent in allowing and providing consequences for your child that God might use? Choose one idea. Implement it all week and discuss it with a trusted person.

*A Biblical View
of Parenting*

God's Glory Is the Preeminent Goal of Parenting

Whether then you eat or drink or whatever you do,
do all to the glory of God.

~ 1 Corinthians 10:31

As a parent, you have goals that guide your decisions. For example, you want a great relationship with your child. You want a well-behaved child. Adoptive parents are often encouraged in intermediate objectives such as healing from past trauma, bonding, or changing the material brain—all to help the child thrive in society. The highest priority of many Christian parents is usually the salvation of their children.

These common goals are good, but insufficient or often wrongly prioritized. Focused on the child and outcomes, they distract from what is most important. What is *God's* goal for parents? What primary aim should preside over parenting decisions?

In 1 Corinthians 10, Paul was writing to people in conflict over whether it was acceptable to eat meat that had been sacrificed to idols. He tells them that the meat isn't the issue. Nor is how others behave. The issue is their goal. "Whether then you eat or drink or whatever you do, do all to the glory of God."

Jesus lived on earth primarily for the glory of God (John 14:13; 17:4). Likewise, we are to serve for the glory of God (1 Peter 4:11). Why? Because He is most worthy and we love Him supremely. "For from Him and through Him and to Him are all things. To Him be the glory forever. Amen" (Romans 11:36).

This universal principle applies to parents also. Whatever you do as a parent, do all to the glory of God. Passion for God's glory must be preeminent. Of course, we should have many objectives for our children. The question is, which is the driver? Are you gentle primarily to gain your child's trust or to please God? Do you discipline primarily because you want a well-behaved child or because you want to heed Scripture? Does the pursuit of relationship hold you back from providing discipline that might anger the child? Do you find yourself more concerned about keeping peace in the household than standing firm on rules?

Certainly, we want our children to know God, but many parents focus so intently on that goal that they press little ones to "pray the salvation prayer." Later, they won't even consider the possibility that a rebellious teen who prayed "the prayer" might not be saved. They grow angry or despairing when their children stray. This reaction indicates outcome-focus. As a parent, you are still a child of God and must rejoice in Christ even if there is grief over a child not saved.

If you consistently seek to glorify God in your parenting, you may have the worst criminal for a child and yet have remained faithful as a parent. If the glory of God is not your preeminent aim, you may have the most well-behaved, Christian child in the world and yet fail as a parent. Parent first and foremost for the glory of God.

Reflection

- Why must the glory of God be a parent's most valued goal?
- What is it about Christ that makes Him most lovable and worthy of glory?
- How can the pursuit of outcomes distract us from keeping the pursuit of God's glory uppermost?
- How does parenting for God's glory first improve the parent's actions and attitudes?

Implementation

- Spend a week evaluating. Log five parenting decisions per day. About each, answer these questions:
  - What were you thinking when you made that particular parenting decision? What were you most wanting to achieve? What were you not wanting to lose?
  - What was of greatest concern: God and His instructions or the child and his responses? Were you focused on behavioral outcomes or obedience to God?
  - In the cases when it was not primarily to please God, what would change if you chose the glory of God as your highest aim? How might you do so? Pray about this.
- Write 1 Corinthians 10:31 on a card and keep it with you. Each time this week you have a disciplinary situation with your child, read the card first, then plan and do what the Word of God instructs in order to glorify God. Log how this changes your attitudes and words.

MEDITATION 13:

Clarify Responsibilities

Fathers shall not be put to death for their sons, nor shall sons be put to death for their fathers; each shall be put to death for his own sin.

~ Deuteronomy 24:16

THE POINT IS, *each person is responsible for his own moral choices.*

How does this help Bessie? She is frustrated because she can't get Donnie to behave. Striving to be a responsible parent, she praises, rewards, reminds (nags), bargains, threatens, and punishes. Nothing works. She wonders, "What am I doing wrong?" She excuses him because, after all, he was "wounded" by pre-adoptive experiences and has a "disorder." She frets in fear that Donnie will grow worse with age and get into serious trouble.

Bessie's struggle with emotions is complicating her situation. If she will filter her situation through Deuteronomy 24:16, she can clarify responsibilities, resulting in less incitement to fear, anger, and manipulation, because she will not be trying to control what she cannot and is not her responsibility.

For example, Ephesians 6:1-4 teaches that parents and children each have distinct responsibilities. Parents are responsible to model ("not provoke"), instruct, and discipline children. Children are responsible to honor and obey parents. It says, "Children, obey . . ." and "Fathers, do not provoke . . ." God did not command parents to make children honor and obey; He commanded children to do it. The child can choose obedience or rebellion and is responsible for his choice. Parents are responsible only to deliver the consequences appropriate to the child's choice, not to sinfully manipulate a child into a behavior.

Disciplining disobedience is not the same as manipulating for obedience. It is simply delivering a (hopefully) influential consequence that comes with the child's responsibility. The fine a driver pays for speeding is a consequence that comes with the responsibility of a driver's license.

What Bessie must accept is that while parenting is influential, it is not determinative. She can influence, but cannot control Donnie's heart. She can't save him or make him behave like a Christian. No matter what she does, he will make his own choices. Parents are absolutely responsible for their influence, but not for how the child responds to their influence.

She must also accept that good parenting does not guarantee a well-behaved child. Ezekiel 18, a chapter on individual responsibility, relates the case of the righteous man whose son turns violent—"His blood will be on his own head" (18:13). Each is responsible for his own choices.

What shall she do? First, she teaches. When he understands, she stops explaining. When he disobeys, she disciplines. She doesn't nag, bargain, or threaten. Rather, she treats Donnie as an intelligent human and trusts God with what is not her responsibility—Donnie's choice to disobey.

Bessie may feel sad over Donnie's foolish choices, but if she refuses to take on Donnie's responsibility, she will be far less angry, manipulating, or despairing. Instead, she can rest satisfied that she carried out her God-given responsibility, even if Donnie does not fulfill his. She does her parenting, lets Donnie choose responses, and calmly delivers the consequences that come with his choices. She devotes herself to faithful parenting and trusts God with the outcome (Proverbs 3:5-6).

- Do *influence* your child's heart by cultivating relationship and applying humble, consistent instruction and discipline.
- Do *not* imagine that you can control your child's heart or force gladly-given good behavior. Those are not in your control, nor are they your responsibility.
- Do diligently deliver the consequences befitting your child's failure to honor and obey, and then leave the outcome between him and God.
- Do accept that you will feel discomfort when your child is unhappy or struggling. It is not your responsibility to fix his feelings.

In summary, obey God in your responsibilities. Trust God with the responsibilities of others.

Reflection

- Do you nag, bargain, or threaten?
- What do you think of the idea that God calls you to be a faithful parent, not to coerce good behavior?
- Do you resist letting your child struggle with difficulties (within his abilities)? Do you excuse him or save him from the consequences of his actions?

Implementation

- For each interaction with your child today, evaluate, "Am I most seeking to obey God or to change my child?"
- Log the times you correctly act in teaching obedience.
- Log the times you withhold appropriate consequences for your child's infractions.

Do Not Provoke Your Child

*Fathers, do not provoke your children to anger, but bring them up in
the discipline and instruction of the Lord.*

~ Ephesians 6:4

As COMPLICATED AS parenting can get, Paul's instruction is helpfully concise—just three injunctions—don't provoke, but discipline, and instruct. We generally understand the discipline and instruct, but what does "do not provoke" mean? In summary, treat your child with respect. Parents can't *make* a child mad, but they can behave in a provoking way and are responsible for their influence. Obey Scripture yourself and you won't unnecessarily irritate or exasperate others.

For example, Donnie's chronic anger originated in his pre-adoption experiences. How can Bert and Bessie help him? One of the first steps is to evaluate their own influence to ensure they are not unwittingly provoking continued anger.

Reflection

Self-evaluation requires humility and willingness to see what we might be missing. The questions below might help. To avoid feeling overwhelmed, answer just one bullet point per day.

- Are you consistently obeying God's Word? Do you submit to authorities without complaint? Parents who live by their own rules are modeling the same autonomy and self-sufficiency that the alienated child practices.
- Do you listen to your child? Do you hear him out when he has a complaint or disagrees with you? Do you interrupt him? Do you ever ask for forgiveness from your child when you have sinned against him?
- Do you spend time just being with your child? Have fun together?
- Are your expectations above his ability? Do your expectations for your child change from day to day? Are rules too restrictive or too loose? Is he allowed to sin without restraint or correction?
- Do you discipline your child for things before telling him the rules? Do you correct him where others can see or hear? Embarrassment is humiliating and unkind.

୬ Do you yell? Nag? Scold and lecture? Constantly find fault? Mimic or mock? Call him names? Accuse? Threaten? Belittle or frequently override his decisions? Withhold affection when he does not cooperate? Do your facial expressions and body language communicate disdain?

୬ Do you stay silent except when he needs correction, or do you encourage him?

୬ Do you show favoritism among the children? Do you compare them?

Implementation

୬ If you have provoked your child, tempting him to a sinful response, do the following:

1. Identify what you have done to provoke your child.
2. Confess sins to God (1 John 1:9). Be specific.
3. Confess sins to your child (Matthew 5:23-24). State specifically what you did, agree that it was wrong, and ask, "Will you forgive me?"
4. Plan how you will change. With what will you replace provoking words or behaviors? What can you do to provoke your children to love (Hebrews 10:24)?
5. Log your change and ask your spouse for feedback.

୬ Invite a church leader or biblical counselor to evaluate your parenting.

MEDITATION 15:

Practice Wise Compassion

*And so, as those who have been chosen of God, holy and beloved, put on
a heart of compassion, kindness, humility, gentleness, and patience ...*

~ Colossians 3:12, NASB

AFTER A DELIGHTFUL week in the Ecuadorian jungle, I suddenly felt anxious, ready to run. Everything seemed strange to me—the living quarters, building construction, language, schedule, climate, foods, companions, and cultural expectations. One night, I distracted myself by staring out a screen-covered window at the noisy jungle. To further escape, I shut my eyes to imagine home and found I couldn't get away from the strange smells and sounds. Opening my eyes, there again were jungle plants rather than maple trees. I felt trapped. It was culture shock.

Consider how different your adopted child's life experiences were from yours—in family and community cultures and environment. Add the fact that his trust has been betrayed. Perhaps he lived with neglect, hunger, filth, abuse, and/or rejection. Add sadness over many losses, ignorance of how to behave, and perhaps neurological deficiencies from malnutrition or drugs in utero. Then he was handed into the care of strangers who took him from all that is familiar. Everything was strange—the terrain, the flora, the climate, the house, food, clothes, sights, smells, people, habits, communication, and cultural expectations. He likely felt overwhelmed, helpless and had no way to assess if he was safe.

Add the perpetual mystery about separation from biological parents and the questions he can't answer. Why was I separated from my mom? Is something wrong with me? Who would I be if I'd stayed with her? How do I handle feeling different from my present family? If I identify with my adoptive family, will I be betraying my birth parents?

Compound it all with the fact that because he has a sinful heart, his perceptions and beliefs about people and mistreatment are distorted. Accordingly, he learned bad habits of all sorts in behavior, thinking, and desires.

Naturally, then, the child you adopted arrived with questions, assumptions, and expectations very different from yours. He thought (and still thinks) differently about issues like safety, authority, parents, identity, right and wrong, pain and suffering, what justice is, handling perceived offenses, outlook on the future, and how to communicate. For example, fearing the pain of further loss, he holds an abiding resistance to connecting with anyone else emotionally. The taproot of these world-view assumptions is the core value of survival. Is it any wonder, then, that your child behaves in ways that are difficult to deal with?

Colossian 3:12 tells us to "put on a heart of compassion, kindness, humility, gentleness, and patience." Compassion feels with another. When Jesus saw distressed people, His compassion moved Him to heal and teach. Similarly, parents need to see life from the adopted child's viewpoint and be moved to reassure, teach, and deal with tough questions wisely. Putting on compassion doesn't mean excusing selfish behavior; tolerating sin produces more trouble for the child. Rather, they lead the child toward godly solutions; that is true kindness. It is done with a low view of self, keeping strength under control, with slowness to anger.

Reflection

- How might efforts to see life as your child sees help your parenting?
- What are some ways you can show compassion without enabling sin or bad habits?
- How does a parent apply compassion in discipline?

Implementation

- Plan compassionate, Bible-based responses to issues in this meditation and discuss with your child. So, what might be grace-giving answers to:
  - What do I do with my sense of loss?
  - How should I perceive my biological mom? How should I perceive my adoptive mom?
  - I don't want to be betrayed again, so I'll reject you before you do me.
- Tell your child that sadness over his past is appropriate, but he can also live in a God-honoring way today.
- Be constantly forgiving the child to show love and to show how God treats His children.
- Settle your child's fears before you instruct.
- Acknowledge your child's feelings before teaching him that he doesn't have to live by feelings and that he can choose thoughts and behaviors regardless of feelings.
- When dealing with inappropriate behaviors that might arise from fear, sadness, or cultural confusion, when he is receptive, explain what a God-trusting action would have been in the situation.

You Don't Have to "Love Enough"

*Jesus replied: "'Love the Lord your God with all your heart, and with
all your soul, and with all your mind.' This is the first and greatest
commandment. And the second is like it: 'Love your neighbor as yourself.'"*

~ Matthew 22:37-39, NIV

WHY DID GOD command foremost that we love Him and others rather
than that we love ourselves? One, God deserves our supreme love.
Two, as the second commandment assumes, we already love ourselves
supremely. We are so selfish that we have to be told to love others, and
love at least as much as we love ourselves.

Some say the heart is an empty cup that needs to be filled with love
before the person can love others. This directly opposes God's commands. Love is self-sacrifice for the welfare of the other. It is what Christ
did when He willingly gave His life so others could receive eternal life.

Parents commonly approach adoption with love-cup theology,
which teaches that children misbehave because, having been abandoned
or traumatized, they don't have enough love. We then assume that if we
love enough, the adopted child will heal and settle into the family. Fill
the love tank and the child will be enabled to reciprocate. If instead,
the child continues to be troublesome, we try harder. For children who
persist in distrust and increasing misbehaviors, parents find that trying
to love enough is like running water into an unplugged sink. It is never
enough. They conclude that the child just can't get enough love.

What if feeling loved isn't the child's goal? What if he most wants a
sense of safety? What if he is craving certainty (that he will never again
lose someone he loves)? Then a full "love cup" is a moot point.

Can any human ever provide "enough love" for another? Some well-
loved children become criminals. Jesus gave infinite love, sacrificing His
own life for others, yet it isn't enough to change most people. Multitudes are loved and well-behaved adults, yet still reject God, the ultimate
source of all love.

People are not constructed with love tanks any more than with joy tanks
or peace tanks. We are born with hearts full of cravings for things we want.
James teaches that the reason we misbehave is to obtain what we want—a
brother's toy, attention, security, etc. (1:14; 3:1-2). Our greatest need is not
feeling loved. Our greatest need is a new, regenerate heart able to love God.

Parent, love God above all. Then love your child as you love yourself, but not to fill a love cup. While you love your child fervently and faithfully, remember that you will never be able to satisfy a child who has insatiable cravings for security and control. Instead, seek to love and please Christ in your parenting. That is what you are commanded to do and what you *can* successfully do. You don't have to love enough; you just need to love like God says to do.

Reflection

- Is there any biblical command to love enough?
- What Bible verse helps you rest in the love of Christ for you?
- Would you be satisfied if your love persuaded your child to reciprocity, good behavior, and a happy family? Would that be enough for you?
- How might dropping the goal of loving enough affect your frustration level, and why?
- What is one way you might teach your child his need to love God more than self?

Implementation

- How does your reason for loving your child compare with Matthew 22:37-39? Talk to God about your motives.
- Are you frequently affirming your child? Ten times today, tell him you love him and wish him well. Reassure him of your desire to keep him safe and cared for. Do this daily.
- Teach or remind your child of the two greatest commandments required of him. Explain the connection of the second command to the first.

Attachment to Christ Is Most Important

So that your trust may be in the LORD,
I have taught you today, even you.

~ Proverbs 22:19, NASB

CHILDREN'S TRUST IN parents is extremely important. The whole trust-based affectional bond is important. A trustful child is calm and teachable. A child who distrusts parents will hold himself apart, question parents' judgment, believe they lie, and oppose them. Therefore, gaining a trust-bond is often viewed as an essential solution. Adoptive parents are urged to make it a regulating priority.

Efforts to establish an affectional bond or relationship are right, good, and important, but setting a bond as the central goal creates problems. One, parents become child-centered. They shape their approach and actions according to whether those actions will persuade the child to bond. Two, parents become adopted-child centered. The non-troublesome siblings are neglected more than parents might realize. Three, it sets up parents for frustration and despair. Affection and trust can't be forced. Simultaneously, the loss of relationship feels catastrophic.

If bonding is the bulls-eye, then the parent is shooting at the wrong target—a man-centered target. Proverbs 22:19 would read, "So that your trust may be in me, your Mom/Dad, I have taught you."

Proverbs shows a God-centered target. Written by a father to his son,[1] Proverbs holds extensive wisdom on many areas of life that promote bonding and human flourishing. However, Proverbs is not for mere self-improvement. Of course the father wants a good relationship. Of course he wants blessings for his son. Yet he states his goal clearly. He most wants his son to trust in the *Lord*.

As Voddie Baucham says, "Ultimately, I'm shepherding my children to the cross. The most important thing with me and my children is not necessarily their finding their way to me, but their finding their way through me to God."[2]

Why is a trust-based affectional bond with God the higher goal? A child's greatest problem is not alienation from parents; it is alienation from God. His problem is not a mental disorder, but a worship disorder.

---

1. Proverbs 1:8, 10, 15; 2:1; 3:1, 11, 21; 4:10, 20; 5:1, 7, 20; 6:1, 3, 20; 7:1, 24; 19:27; 23:15, 19, 26; 24:21
2. Voddie Baucham, *Rooted*, Hope for Orphans International, 2016, p. 20.

The cause is not distrust of parents, but trust in self. He is a sinner who needs forgiveness, salvation, and an eternal, trust-based relationship with Jesus.

Bonding as an intermediary that enhances the child's openness to hearing the gospel is a powerful aid toward the bulls-eye, but only an intermediary. Although trust in parents is a potent influence, nowhere does the Bible command parents to get children to bond or trust them. He commands that parents love their children, model godliness, instruct, and discipline. These practices influence children toward God. We want them to listen to their parents because they need to hear and heed the gospel.

We parents certainly should be trustworthy and cultivate relational connection. We rightly hope our children will trust us. We hope they will develop an affectional bond with us. But we cannot make them do so. Teaching and inducing trust in God is where the energy of parents should be directed.

"So that your trust may be in the LORD, I have taught you today ..." (Proverbs 22:19, NASB).

Reflection

- 🖎 What do you think of Mr. Baucham's statement?
- 🖎 Based on your words and actions, what would your child say you most want for him—to trust God or to trust you?
- 🖎 How does believing the gospel result in attachment to God?
- 🖎 What is lovable about Christ? Why would anyone trust and obey Christ when life is so hard or when it means possibly losing one's safety or happiness? Why risk trusting God instead of self?

Implementation

- 🖎 What do you do to cultivate your relationship with Christ? How can you improve?
- 🖎 Plan three short statements intended to show your child the lovableness of Christ or to help him become aware of his need for Christ. Use one or another in moments when he is teachable.

Train Diligently; Trust Determinedly

Train up a child according to his way,
Even when he is old he will not depart from it.

~ Proverbs 22:6

HOW MANY TIMES Bessie has heard, "Train up a child in the way he should go, even when he is old he will not depart from it" (NASB)! So if she loves enough and parents well, her child will eventually behave well. People even cite the verse and add, "Some day your child will thank you." But Bessie finds that nothing she does works. She can't make Donnie behave. She thinks, "What am I doing wrong? If Proverbs 22 is right, I must be a bad mom."

With an incorrect view of Proverbs 22:6, Bessie has unwittingly shifted to pragmatism. If Mom does this then the outcome will be that. If it isn't, she tries nagging or threats or some new method (for the child's good!). This is behavioristic parenting, and her pragmatism results in self-doubt, worry, anger, conflicts, and unnecessary guilt.

A right understanding will help. More literal to the Hebrew, Proverbs 22:6 says, "Dedicate a child upon the mouth of his way . . ." In other words, if allowed to go the way *he says he wants* to go, the child will practice his foolishness and selfishness into habits. The LSB captures the Hebrew with, ". . .according to his way." Proverbs 29:15b states the same idea, "a child *left to himself* brings shame to his mother" (emphasis mine). Underlying the point are assumptions on child development:

- Having an independent will, children are not just passive receivers, but active choosers.
- Having inherent desires, children choose ways they want to go regardless of parental influence.
- Inherently sinful and foolish, children are not good and wise; no one has to teach them to be selfish or foolish.
- Habitual beings, children form habits, habits of desires, thoughts, and behaviors.

The point of the verse is not what is so commonly tossed out in conversations, that a rebellious child of good parents will one day come to his senses. The point is that *habits built in youth continue into adulthood.* These may be habits he teaches himself as much as those taught by parents. Good or bad, the habits he practices will stick with him.

Therefore, while parental influence is extremely important, it is *not* determinative. Children are not just malleable clay. They possess wills of their own corrupted by sin. Some children of loving, wise parents secretly cultivate ungodly desires and attitudes that become apparent only when the child is brave enough and capable to act in opposition to parents. Unless God intervenes, the Proverbs 22:6 principle of habituation predicts that the child's self-practiced habits of heart will override godly parental influence.

Therefore, one lesson for parents is to diligently train their children, but not as a guarantee or formula for good behavior. Parents are stewards, not masters. Train hearts, not just behaviors. Cultivate right desires such as love for God and others, love of wisdom, and the attitude that we're here to serve, not be served.

A second lesson is to trust God determinedly, determinedly because temptations to worry, anger, sinful manipulation, or unnecessary guilt are likely. Our children's hearts are not in our control, but they are in God's control. Therefore, we influence as we can and then leave the results in God's hands.

Parenting is influential, not determinative. Train diligently; trust determinedly.

Reflections

- ❧ How does a right understanding of Proverbs 22:6 steer a parent away from pragmatic behaviorism and toward diligence as a steward?
- ❧ What does it mean that parenting is not determinative? Why does this truth require determination in trusting God? How does it offer hope?
- ❧ Parents may rightly take credit for their influence. How much credit may they rightly take for what a child did with that influence? How does this relate to parental pride over a child's success or guilt over persistent misbehavior?

Implementation

- ❧ Write a prayer committing to train diligently more as a steward under God than for obtaining results from the child. How will this commitment affect your responses to his misbehavior?
- ❧ Regarding your child, for what do you need to trust God more? What will you do to practice trusting?

Talk Less

When there are many words, transgression is unavoidable,
But he who restrains his lips is wise.

~ Proverbs 10:19, NASB

HAVE YOU NOTICED how your child's eyes glaze over when you go on and on about something or say it over and over, day after day? Why do moms use so many words? Isn't it because we want the child to do what we say—to do the right thing?

Proverbs says that "when there are many words, transgression is unavoidable." How so? Some people love to hear themselves far more than others want to hear them (pride). Or, some people use words to dominate a conversation, staying center stage or preventing others from sharing opposing ideas.

When it comes to child-rearing, parents often repeat or lecture to persuade. Throw many words at someone and he might finally agree or just give up and do what is good for him. Parents usually mean well with all their talk.

Actually, nagging is manipulative and disrespectful because it communicates, "I don't accept your choice, so I will punish you with words until you do what I want." It is also foolish because many words plug the ears.

"He who restrains his lips is wise." You will not be heard for your many words; you'll be rejected. So, once the child knows what you're teaching, don't harp on it, not even if he refuses to change.

Your child is smart. He knows what you said. Teach, check for understanding, then hold accountable for what is known. Instead of repeating, act. Deliver the consequences that accompany his choice. This demonstrates respect. In this case, actions speak louder than words. After you act, recheck for understanding, then again expect compliance.

What about spiritual training? Naturally, you long for the salvation of your children. Can your many gospel words save him? Might they not cause him to stumble into the sin of anger at you for needlessly frustrating him? Does nagging make our Lord attractive or repulsive?

The wise restrain speech. In this way, they do not fall into sin nor tempt others to sin.

Say it concisely. Give a command once and be done. Talk less.

Reflection

- ℘ When someone insists on repeating to you something you already know, how do you feel about it?
- ℘ Why do many words lead the speaker into transgression?
- ℘ How does restraining speech demonstrate wisdom?

Implementation

- ℘ For one week observe yourself in your conversations with people. Who talks more, you or the other? Who is asking questions that promote the other to speak? If you find yourself talking a lot, plan how to restrain your lips. Practice it and observe results in relationships.
- ℘ With your child, clearly state your expectation. If he doesn't do it, discipline *before* you repeat the command, *if* you repeat at all. For one week, log how many times you handle infractions this way. Evaluate and plan how to improve.
- ℘ When you explain the gospel, have the child explain it back to you. Record the date you conclude that he understands it. After that, periodically (semiannually?) ask a single question about one aspect or another to check his understanding. (This will inform you about whether the child knows the gospel and what you do and do *not* need to reteach. A longer conversation is fine, so long as you don't lecture and rehearse to his irritation.)

God Does the Saving

But God, being rich in mercy because of His great love with which He loved us, even when we were dead in our transgressions, made us alive together with Christ—by grace you have been saved.

~ Ephesians 2:4-5

"GRACE" IS GOD interjecting Himself into the life of an undeserving sinner to save or, after salvation, to enable obedience (1 Corinthians 15:9-10). Why is salvation by grace? Because people are born dead in sin, and the dead cannot do anything, let alone respond rightly to God. It is God who gives life. "According to God's great mercy He has caused us to be born again" (1 Peter 1:3). Considering our sin, it is amazing that He makes anyone alive with Christ. He is indeed rich in mercy and great in love!

Bessie is fervently grateful that God made her alive with Christ. Loving her son, she intensely wants the same for Donnie. His eternity is at stake! She and Bert pray, have family devotions, attend church, and share the gospel to that end. However, while Donnie charms his teachers and prays the sinner's prayer in different church venues, he is growing more incorrigible. Bessie recites the gospel to him every day and frequently tries to persuade him to genuinely repent. Church attendance has become less about worship and more about providing influence on Donnie.

In her increasing worry, frustration, and efforts, what Bessie may not realize is that she is not accepting that it is God who does the saving. Her sense of responsibility is commendable, but she is pushing beyond her God-given limits. Not by the will of man, Donnie's salvation is not in her control (John 1:13). God doesn't need her!

Certainly, salvation is a good desire! She and Bert *should* influence their children toward loving God. However, worry demonstrates a lack of both trust and submission, doubting "His great love" and rich mercy. Nagging, belaboring, and arguing are disrespectful, demonstrating a lack of love toward her son. When we're willing to sin over something good, the good desire has become sinful because it is more valued than is God's will. She must submit to God's will that Donnie is not yet saved.

Repeating the gospel is not the solution because Donnie's problem is not a lack of hearing or memory. It is a lack of sight. Mothers are incapable of opening blind eyes.

What can Bessie do? She can influence for Christ and leave the saving to God. For example, once she knows her son understands the truths of the gospel, she won't harp on it. She may check his understanding periodically, but she will *respect* her son's intelligence and choice.

What about her extreme desire? Bessie has an opportunity to love and trust the One who has loved her enough to die for her. She must choose to want the will of God more than her own will. That means living in a tension. While she rightly wants and prays for Donnie's salvation, she also entrusts it to God and loves Him *even if her child is never saved.*

Reflection

- How has God been rich in mercy toward you?
- What is your view of your role in the salvation of your child?
- What have you done to influence your child to see the value of Christ? How might you have done too much and be exasperating your child?
- What is your response to this statement: For the salvation of my child, God doesn't need me.
- Parents can have various motives for wanting a child's salvation— God's glory, the child's blessing, the parent's reputation, reduced conflicts, etc. How might you assess your motives?

Implementation

- By observing behavior and gently asked questions in teachable moments, evaluate whether your child understands who Christ is and the gospel. Then you'll know what, if anything, still needs to be clarified.
- Log how often you say something evangelistic. If an atheist was trying to persuade you toward atheism in the ways you are trying to persuade your child toward Christ, how would you feel?
- What do you need to change (or continue) to demonstrate respect to your child and trust in God?

A Mother's Attitudes

The Question Isn't "Why?"

"If you love Me, you will keep My commandments …
He who has My commandments and keeps
them is the one who loves Me."

~ John 14:15, 21a

THESE WORDS ARE from Jesus' last sermon of Proverbs 25:28. After three years of hard work proclaiming the good news of salvation, He had very few followers—just His beloved disciples. Even they would soon abandon Him as He was arrested, tortured, and died a humiliating death on the cross. In confusion and despair over these events, the disciples must have wondered, "Why would God have Jesus' life and years of faithful ministry end in futility?" Even so, Jesus had called them to obedience, not to explanations. "He who has My commandments and keeps them, He it is who loves Me."

A parent's grief may be great when a child continues in alienation and rebellion year after year with increasing resolve. The parent tries endlessly to demonstrate love and to draw the child into relationship. If that doesn't work, as she senses the child pulling away with escalating determination, she feels the loss of the relationship she craved, loss of the dream of the kind of family she wanted, and heartache over watching her child on a self-destructive trajectory. The breaks in her heart ooze sadness.

Nothing has worked. It seems all for naught. Having done all she could to honor God, the problems have not been solved. It doesn't make sense. Would God want her child to end up jobless? Homeless? On the street? Possibly, a criminal? At the futility of it all, the tendency is to despair and to wonder what God is doing, even to ask, "Why? I poured into the child all of my commitment, love, strength, thoughts, finances, and prayers. Why isn't it bearing fruit? Why do I have to lose one I sacrificed so much to adopt and raise? Why is God taking this child from me?"

A better question is "who?" A right view of God is the ground for godly suffering.

The next question is "what?" As a missionary widow in severe loss and seeming futility, Elisabeth Elliott, observed for herself that despair is actually exacerbated by a demand to know the why.[1] It can't be answered

---

1. Ellen Vaughn. *Becoming Elisabeth Elliot.* (Nashville, Tennessee: B&H Publishing Group, 2020), 261-62.

and the answer would never satisfy. She proposes that the question to ask is "what?" I would add that the right "what" question is not "What is the Lord trying to teach me?"

It is right to grieve for a time, but staying in grief will not help. The key to navigating the grief and confusion is not understanding God's reasons, but obeying His commands. "What does the Word of God say to do now?" Right responses produce hope.

At this point, there is an essential "why" question for a Christian to answer. "Why obey God?" The answer lies in Jesus' last sermon, "He who has My commandments and keeps them, he it is who loves Me." Don't obey out of legalism or gutting through grief. Rather, remember how much Christ has done for you and love Him back with trust and obedience. Because we love our Lord who loves us, we trust and obey moment by moment. While acknowledging the pain of loss and grief, the important question is not "Why did this happen?" but "What shall I do in love for my Father so that He will be glorified in my situation?"

Reflection

- In adversity, why does knowing why provide a sense of control? Does knowing why lessen the pain?
- In the Bible God has given several reasons for suffering in general. How does *not* knowing the "why" for your *particular* trial build faith?

Implementation

- Has grief or despair taken the wind out of your sails? Read John 14:15 and 21. Identify the next thing you need to do today. Do it in love to Christ.
- Choose a verse that comforts you. Write it on a card and tape it to your cabinet door. When sadness hits you like a wrecking ball, read the verse and talk to God about your sadness, using the verse in your prayer.

Discipline Guards the Mind

Like *a city that is broken into* and *without a wall*
Is a man without restraint over his spirit.

~ Proverbs 25:28

NUMBERS 13 AND 14 record a real-life example. Preparing to enter the promised land, Moses sent twelve men to reconnoiter. Returning, all reported its fruitfulness. So far so good. Then ten warned of supersized inhabitants "and we became like grasshoppers in our own sight" (Numbers 13:33). Caleb countered, "With God we can overcome." Everybody wailed, "Giants in the land! We're going to die! The world is ending!" (paraphrased). Minimizing God, they characterized the danger as worse than it was and refused to enter.

Proverbs 25:28 says that someone who doesn't control his spirit is like a city without walls An ancient city without walls was vulnerable to being plundered. Under attack, citizens had to run for cover or be enslaved or slaughtered. Likewise, thoughts running wild in the mind disrupt true, orderly, productive thinking. Perspective becomes warped, leading to misjudgments which produce actions inappropriate to the situation. Your mental city needs walls. Discipline guards the mind.

While odd and oppositional behaviors in a newly adopted child are understandable, if, despite years of loving attention and appropriate discipline, behaviors digress to the bizarre, manipulative, and malicious, a parent may feel surprised and confused. This isn't how adoption is supposed to work. If parents listen to their emotions, misbehaviors loom darker or more catastrophic than they are, which incites overreaction.

Bessie, for example, keeps being shocked by Donnie's extreme and unremitting misbehavior. While it is commendable that she assumes the best of him, surprise and shock keep her anxious and unsure of how to respond, interfering with calm, wise responses. Donnie sees her surprise as a rewarding effect and her uncertainty as a weakness to exploit.

Feelings and perceptions are not the sources of truth; the Word of God is. But we will believe the Word over perceptions only if we discipline ourselves to do so. Self-discipline of emotions and thoughts is the wall that guards the mind.

For example, surprise at wickedness in a child arises from a failure to grasp the doctrine of depravity. The truth is, like the best and worst humans, your child has a heart prone to evil, that produces sinful behaviors. Extreme misbehaviors, even bizarre behaviors in children should be no surprise to the Christian. To perceive misbehavior in a way that leads to the gospel, parents must choose the biblical view of sin.

When we view God through our trouble rather than the trouble through God, the trouble looms larger than God. This is not realistic. Rather than be surprised at how outrageous the child's behavior is, assess the situation biblically. Calmly keep responding in a godly manner—prayerfully, calmly, speaking truth gently without condemnation in face or voice, providing appropriate consequences consistently and unwaveringly. Do grieve as appropriate, but don't perceive it to be darker than it is. Move on in continued obedience to Christ.

Reflection

- If Bessie's reaction is also true of you, what underlies your continued surprise at misbehaviors? Is it from the under-appreciation of sin's influence on children? Is it your resistance to having your hopes for a family dashed? Is it something else?
- How does shock in reaction to a child's misbehavior affect your ability to think and respond biblically and clearly?

Implementation

- If you are prone to alarm, search the Scriptures to learn what God says about it. Find a friend to consult to help you gain a more realistic perspective of the present situation.
- Formulate a plan for how to handle particular behaviors of your child, then work the plan.
- List truths to tell yourself when you begin to feel anxious. For example, "God is sovereign. My child is not outside His control." Or, "God is loving. If I lose the love of my child, I will still have the love of God."

When Anxious, Fear the Lord

How blessed is the man who fears Yahweh,
Who greatly delights in His commandments...
He will not fear an evil report;
His heart is set, trusting in Yahweh.

~ Psalm 112:1, 7

ANXIETIES CHURN OVER thoughts of the future, not past or present. What if the doctor calls with bad news? What if I lose my job? What if my child rejects me?... ends up homeless?... never becomes a Christian? Worry thoughts are attempts to control the future by thoughts in the present. What-ifs and worries don't work because they have no power to change tomorrow. Instead, they produce depression. "Anxiety in a man's heart weighs it down" (Proverbs 12:25a).

Psalm 112:7 says the godly man does not fear what might happen tomorrow. Why? He fears the Lord. Aware of being a mere creature, he submits to the fact that God will do with him what *God* decides. He carries a mingled dread of sin's consequences and joyful love for God who blesses. Since we fear displeasing those we love, a right fear of God motivates glad obedience.

How does fear of the Lord relate to anxiety?

- Delighting in God's command to trust Him, when worry tempts us, we gladly "set" our hearts to trustfully accept circumstances we can't change (Psalm 112:1, 7).
- In love for God, we treat worry as sin. Acting as though God is not good and not in control, worry practices unbelief. Since love believes (assumes) the best (1 Corinthians 13:7), doubting God's goodness should prick the Christian's heart.
- Since a greater fear dispels a lesser fear, if you are most concerned about pleasing God, concerns about adversarial possibilities won't have room in your thoughts. "His heart is upheld, he will not fear, until he looks with satisfaction on his adversaries" (Psalm 112:8).

So how do you *do* trust? What does trust in God look like?

When tempted to worry, remind yourself to believe the best of God, that He will work good from anything that might happen.

Repent quickly of worry thoughts. As soon as you catch yourself thinking unproductively about the future, confess unbelief and focus on God-honoring thoughts. Treating worry as sin may sound harsh, but it actually builds hope because it reminds you that you don't *have* to worry. You can be free! There is a way out and you know what it is—obedience. (This is the same hope you can offer your child.)

"Greatly delight in His commandments." The question is not "what if?" but, "what obedience is required now?" Despite the threats, fearing God more, the psalmist worked for income, did what was right, and gave to others (Psalm 112:1, 3-5, 9). As Jesus said, "Stop worrying about food or tomorrow. Since God already lovingly promises to meet all your needs, leave that to Him and trustfully busy yourself thinking and working on His agenda" (Matthew 6:25-33). Loving God and neighbor *now*, you don't have time to worry about *tomorrow*.

It can be very hard to let go of worrisome thoughts about our children. However, doing so practices full trust in God and prevents despair. You aren't being an unloving mother because you refuse to sin in worry. You are loving God.

Blessed is the man who fears Yahweh (Psalm 112:1). You are loved by a sovereign God. Believe it in action. Rest on His love and sovereignty. While you *work* to direct your thoughts toward today's responsibilities, *rest* in letting your thoughts be thinking well of God.

Fear the Lord. Determine to trust. Live out that trust.

Reflection

- What concerns (if any) keep cycling through your thoughts? What do you fear might (or might not) happen?
- What will it take to make your heart "steadfast" in trust?
- What means does God provide for upholding the trustful heart?
- How does focus on today's obedience dissipate worries?

Implementation

- List three of your present, personal responsibilities. Fulfill one now.
- List five verses for meditation on the greatness of God. Choose one to think about—who, what, how, why, how much, etc. What response is appropriate? Next week, choose another and do the same.
- List two God-honoring thoughts you can tell yourself when you are tempted to worry.
- Choose a hymn or spiritual song of praise and thanksgiving. Sing it (with gusto) five times today.

When Angry, Walk by the Spirit

*But I say, walk by the Spirit and you will not
carry out the desire of the flesh.*

~ Galatians 5:16

CHILDREN ARE PRECIOUS, but sometimes those sweet little cherubs get the bit in their teeth and run the wagon of your day right into the ditch. Your child may even be deliberately trying to provoke you to anger. There you are in messy circumstances, emotions heating up, and you remember, that you shall love your neighbor as yourself (Galatians 5:14). How can you do it?

Paul answers in verse 16, "Walk by the Spirit, and you will not carry out the desire of the flesh." But your angry desire is at war with your desire to please God. Stresses have built and you feel frustration swelling like a volcano into an angry outburst.

"But the fruit of the Spirit is love, joy, peace, patience, kindness, goodness, faithfulness, gentleness, self-control" (5:22-23). If you do these you will be walking in the Spirit. And yet, provoked repeatedly, it seems impossible. Again, how?

"By the Spirit" means obedience by His power. It requires submission to what the Spirit says *in the Word of God*, obeying no matter how you feel. A walk is an ongoing practice made up of many decisions—to love, to speak kindly, to discipline each time so as to be consistent, and to control yourself. Walking is progressive, meaning the submission is practiced decision by decision into a habitual lifestyle.

In the moment of a child's insubordination, here's what it might look like: You begin the day praying you will practice "love, joy, peace, patience ..." Your child is repeatedly resisting you despite your practice of consistent calm, appropriate, self-controlled corrective action at the first infraction. You have been practicing gentle truth-speaking along the way. Another incident happens and suddenly you want to explode. Stop and pray, "Lord, help!" Applying self-control, you might walk away to another room and pray,

"Lord, I confess my anger as sinful. Please help me to want Your will more than mine. I choose right now to depend on Your Spirit for strength to pray and obey no matter what I feel. I choose to thank You for this opportunity to practice Christlike character. I choose to love my child by asserting gentleness and self-control as I walk back into that room and deal with my child kindly and gently even while I firmly enforce consequences. I am trusting that as I reengage with my child Your Spirit will empower me to practice Galatians 5:23 character."

Then, you walk out there determined to obey, trusting the Spirit to enable that obedience. See what He works in your heart as you do!

Others may apply the intent of the passage differently, but perhaps this gets you started. The point is, decision by decision, obey the Word of God, trusting the Spirit to give you the power to do so. "Walk by the Spirit and you will not carry out the desire of the flesh."

Reflection

- How does practicing the fruit of the Spirit demonstrate that a person is being led by the Spirit?
- Understanding the meaning of the text is not enough. We must *do* it. What do you do to implement Galatians 5:16 in specific situations?

Implementation

- Log your angry thoughts for five days. Observe the three most common. Find scripture verses that address or correct each thought. Write corresponding, Scripture-based God-honoring thoughts and use those to replace the angry thoughts.
- Log three times this week when you consciously implemented this passage, loving in action by the power of the Spirit.

MEDITATION 25:

When Misunderstood, God Knows and Understands

O Yahweh, You have searched me and known me.
You know when I sit down and when I rise up;
You understand my thought from afar.
You scrutinize my path and my lying down,
And are intimately acquainted with all my ways.

~ Psalm 139:1-3

BEING OMNISCIENT, GOD knows everything about you, from the hairs on your head to the thoughts in your head. He knows what you do and when and why. He regulates every situation that influences you.

Your situation might be that of an adoptive parent. A well-adjusted adopted child is a beautiful thing. Many do not adjust well and their parents often find themselves misunderstood. They have endured a degree of ingratitude, opposition, rejection, reviling, bizarre behavior, and perhaps even destructive behavior from a child that most people will never glimpse. Seeking answers, they confide in a friend or church leader. Often, the response shows a lack of understanding and (kindly-intentioned) blame. Behavior, as described, is either the parent's exaggeration or the parent's fault. No child would do such things.

Being misunderstood is difficult to handle. Just when you most need compassionate care and wise counsel, you find your problem compounded by disbelief, blame, and no one to help. Some such parents have even been falsely accused of child abuse and lost jobs. Feeling alone in your troubles exacerbates the pain and gnaws away hope. It can tempt you to self-pity.

Jesus was misunderstood. The crowds misunderstood. His friends and neighbors did not understand. His family thought He was crazy. Jesus was misunderstood by everyone. He knows what it is like (John 12:16; Mark 6:3; 3:21).

Being misunderstood provides you an opportunity to trust God more and seek His counsel in the Word of God. For example, while misunderstood, you are not a special case because "No temptation has overtaken you but such as is common to man" (1 Corinthians 10:13). Multitudes of others in trials have been misunderstood. If you think you are misunderstood, think about how your struggling adopted child feels.

God's omniscience provides the comfort that, even when no one else understands, He does. Knowing that you are understood by the One who most matters, trust Him and set yourself to serve Him despite being misunderstood. A few actions that can help include the following:

- Accept that you might be misunderstood. Some children's behaviors are beyond the experience of most parents and most church leaders. They controvert the cultural rationale that children would be fine if parents would just treat them rightly. They contradict an ideal about children that we all want to believe.
- Identify a couple of friends willing to listen and learn. Make those your confidantes. Be willing to listen and heed their counsel (Proverbs 27:17).
- Take your focus off a sense of isolation. Get busy loving and serving others.

Reflection

- How does viewing one's trial as particularly unique from others hinder spiritual growth? How does it hinder robust fellowship?
- How is the doctrine of God's omniscience a comfort?
- How can you help your local church respond biblically to you?

Implementation

- Limit what you tell the majority of people. If they don't understand, your descriptions make them uncomfortable in ways that are not helpful to them or you.
- As appropriate, provide your confidante with a response that helps him/her: "It's understandable that you don't know what to say to me right now. You could just say, 'I'm sorry for your pain. How can I pray for you?'"
- Refuse to view your case as special or unique.

What if Your Husband Doesn't Understand?

In the same way, you wives, be subject to your own husbands so that even if any of them are disobedient to the word, they may be won without a word by the behavior of their wives, as they observe your chaste and respectful behavior. Your adornment must ... be the hidden person of the heart, with the imperishable quality of a gentle and quiet spirit, which is precious in the sight of God.

~ 1 Peter 3:1-6, NASB

EVERY DAY WHEN Bert comes home from work, Bessie tells him a litany of Donnie's misbehaviors. She is hoping he'll say something like, "Honey, I didn't see the event, but you did. I'm going to take your word for it. How can I help?" Instead, he respectfully listens, but doesn't believe her. She feels frustrated that he sides with Donnie.

Consider Bert's view. He and Bessie adopted Donnie to give him a happy home and influence him for Christ. When he comes home from work, Bert wants to enjoy his children, not deal with disciplinary issues. Donnie behaves well when Bert is around so he can't be as bad as Bessie describes. She is exaggerating because she's tired. She expects too much.

Bessie knows Bert is a good dad but, watching Donnie deceive him, she feels alone in her difficulty. She realizes that if Bert doesn't see the problem, he won't take action to support her authority and protect the siblings. Unable to persuade him, she feels helpless to prevent Donnie from exploiting power gained from having Dad's support.

Alienated adopted children commonly target the mom in particular. Because behavior improves significantly when Dad is around, it is not unusual for an adoptive dad to be unaware and doubt his wife's perspective. What is a wife to do when her husband doesn't understand and take corrective action?

Peter speaks to wives who had unbelieving, even oppressive husbands. He said to win them to Christ more by behavior than by words. Although Peter wrote regarding unbelieving husbands, the principles of a wife's character hold with Christian husbands also.

Behavior must be godly and respectful, flowing from a heart that is gentle, quiet, and fearless. "Gentle" means strength under control. Keeping emotions under control requires the humility of accepting God's dealings with us as good, and taking hardships as God's tools for growth. "Quiet" means to keep your seat, remain undisturbed and not disturbing others, unruffled and unworried.[1] Fearlessness requires trusting that God, sovereign and good, having placed her in submission to an imperfect authority, is more than capable of overruling and working the difficulties for His glory and her good.

Peter grounds his counsel on the example of Christ (1 Peter 2:20-25). While Jesus suffered reviling and the cross, He did not fight back, but kept entrusting Himself to the Father. "Likewise, wives . . ."

When your husband doesn't understand, when you feel alone handling a difficult child, follow He who suffered for you. Like Christ, seek your husband's welfare. Fearing the Lord, keep your behavior excellent. Humbly accept your circumstance as God's good will for you. Keep your heart seated and peaceable. Pray that God gives your husband discernment. Entrusting yourself to God, respectfully appeal to your husband, then submit to his leadership. While being understood and supported makes life easier, your responsibility is not to be loved but to love.

Reflection

- Describe a time when you accepted hardship as God dealing with you for good.
- When your husband doubts your perception or makes mistakes (in your viewpoint), how do you respond? How does it compare with 1 Peter 3:1-6?
- What difference does the example of Christ make when you feel alone in difficulties?

Implementation

- Affirm your husband's good parenting.
- Don't bombard him with daily recitations of the child's infractions. Choose key incidents and ask his counsel on how to deal with it.
- When your husband is home and a disciplinary situation arises, ask him to deal with it. Don't interfere or criticize. Thank him. Pray for him.
- If parenting is a point of serious contention between you, seek counsel from your pastor or a biblical counselor.

---

1. *Strong's Exhaustive Concordance*, https://biblehub.com/greek/2272.htm (Accessed November 18, 2022). For more discussion of quietness of spirit see also Jeremiah Burroughs, *The Rare Jewel of Christian Contentment*, (Edinburgh, UK: The Banner of Truth Press, 1964), 22-31.

Feeling Isolated? God Never Forsakes

…God has said, "Never will I leave you; never will I forsake you."

~ Hebrews 13:5, NIV

IT WAS IN care group that Bessie first admitted her doubts publicly. She and her husband had adopted Donnie a few years earlier with high hopes. They had poured into him the same relational efforts they did with their biological children, and more. Generally, her children appear to be normal.

Yet, Bessie has been sensing something is off. At first, she doubted her perceptions. Only gradually has she been willing to admit to herself that Donnie is not as connected to the family as Bessie had thought, that she feels an emotional distance from Donnie that is not normal; he subtly and abnormally holds himself apart from the family. Unable to connect as a mother should, Bessie feels confused, with a nagging sadness and a growing concern.

Complicating Bessie's concern is the sense of isolation. When she confided in some moms at church, she observed various responses. "It's just a stage." "You need to understand children better." "You expect too much; don't be so hard on the child." "If you just love enough the child will thank you some day."

Also, her church promotes adoption. How can she let them down by admitting it isn't going well? Bessie sees no one to help fight discouragement.

Donnie's case is mild. Some adopted children behave in shocking ways. Parents quickly learn that others cannot imagine that a child could do what this mom says her child does, and figure that bizarre and destructive behaviors must be the parents' fault. They do not understand what it is like to have such an alienated child. So the parents isolate. They may participate in church, but tell no one the torment this child causes in the home to both parents and siblings.

One of the most precious possessions of the Christian is God's abiding presence. No matter what your feelings tell you, if you are a child of God you are never alone. God is always with you.

Delight first in the companionship of Christ. Listen to Him by meditating on His Word. Talk to Him with thanksgiving, praise, and songs. Live out the relationship by obedience in trust with joy. The psalmist says, "the nearness of God is my good" (Psalm 73:28). None can satisfy like Him.

Fellowship with other believers is important and even commanded, but if at times there is no one else, Jesus is enough. He is more than enough. Only He can truly satisfy your heart longings. God has said, "Never will I leave you; never will I forsake you."

Reflection

- ❧ When feeling lonely where do you turn first, to another person or to God in prayer?
- ❧ Meditate on Hebrews 13:5 and for one week log how that verse influences your thoughts or words.

Implementation

- ❧ List what can you do today to enjoy Christ and increase your delight in Him. Choose one idea and do it.
- ❧ Refuse to isolate. Determine one or two ways besides the regular worship service in which you can participate in church life and serve. There may be no one who understands your home life, but you can still participate in mutually encouraging relationships.
- ❧ Refuse to isolate. Inform your pastor and request that an elder, a deacon, or a biblical counselor or advocate be assigned to support you. While most do not understand how radically alienated adopted children can be, don't underestimate and assume they can't help in some way. Tell them what you need. Ask them to educate themselves on adoption issues. (Perhaps give them a book and a website address.[1]) Who knows, maybe one of these people has worked with a case like yours.
- ❧ Refuse to isolate. Invite church members into your home. They will get to know and trust you.

---

1. See the resources at the end of the book. Those particular to better understanding how extreme the behavior of an adopted child can become include my book *(Parenting the Difficult Child)*, and my blog at seedsownpress.wordpress.com. Do online searches on "Reactive Attachment Disorder" and adoption issues. Just be aware most hits speak from a secular psychology worldview.

When Despairing, Talk to Your Heart

Why are you in despair, O my soul? ...
Hope in God, for I shall again praise Him ...

~ Psalm 42:5, 11, NASB

PSALM 42:3 SAYS, "My tears have been my food day and night." The psalmist is hurting! He used to be a happy, socially involved man and a joyful worship leader. Then, for some reason, family and friends began shunning him. Now, some are taunting him "all day long." Scorn has doused his joy and sapped his energy. No one understands. He feels abandoned, forgotten even by God. Troubled thoughts and tears prevent sleep. Joy is gone. Despair has come (42:4, 6, 9).

But he refuses to stay there. How does he move out of despair? He stops listening to his feelings and starts talking to his heart.

"Why are you in despair, O my soul?
And *why* have you become disturbed within me?
Hope in God, for I shall again praise Him
For the help of His presence." (Psalm 42:5, 11, NASB)

Rather than commiserate with his low feelings, he challenges his heart. He stops looking at circumstances and looks to God. Reminding himself of reasons to rejoice, he sees that hope is reasonable because God is present, aware, and overruling. "Help" is a translation of the Hebrew word for "salvation." Anticipating salvation, he can be confident of a brighter future. Applications might be summarized:

- Don't listen to your heart; talk to it.
- Don't listen to your feelings; listen to God (as He speaks in the written Word).
- Don't stop there; get busy with hope.

When a chronically misbehaving child is being especially difficult, a parent can face rebellion and taunts "all day long." Efforts to bless are rejected. There is sadness over the loss of relationship, over a child on the road to trouble, over a sense of ineffectiveness or failure at parenting. When others don't understand, a sense of isolation is added. Despair pounds on the heart's door, and even barges in.

It might seem like sadness is your food day and night, but God is with you and one day you will praise Him with exquisite joy. So when you are feeling low you must challenge your heart. You can echo the psalmist:

"Why are you in despair, O my soul? ...

Hope in God, for I shall again praise Him ..." (Psalm 42:5, 11)

What might this look like? Talk to yourself to stop the trend, listen to God by reading His Word, talk to God about what He says in His Word, then act on it.

Reflection

- How does God's presence comfort and help?
- Why is hope in God reasonable?
- What is it about Christ that gives you hope?

Implementation

- Talk to yourself: Step from the tense situation and ask yourself:
  - Is God sovereign?
  - Is God good?
  - Does God love me?
  - So, even if God ordains hard things, it is for my good.
  - Therefore, what can I do now to trust God and please Him in my situation?
- Listen to God: From a psalm like 13, 16, 18, 46, 85, or 86, slowly read a few verses by those who have gone through similar seasons of life.
  - What does it say?
  - What did it mean to the original audience?
  - What are the implications for me?
  - What is one way I can implement an implication?
- Talk to God. Pray using the psalm. For example, possible prayers from Psalm 86 might include (scripture quotes in italics):
  - "Hear me, Lord, *and answer me because I feel so discouraged.*"
  - "*You are good and ready to forgive and abundant in lovingkindness to all who call upon You.* I'm calling right now. My thoughts are in a jumble, so please help me collect them."
  - "I trust You and I commit to obey Your Word instead of my feelings, so right now, *I will give thanks to You. . .with all my heart ... For Your lovingkindness toward me is great ...*"
- Act on your hope. A thankful heart will drive away despair and anger.
  - List five reasons to rejoice, then use them in thanking and praising God. Do this daily for one month.
  - Carry out your next responsibility.

After Failure, Wipe Off and Walk On

But the path of the righteous is like the light of dawn,
That shines brighter and brighter until the fullness of day.
The way of the wicked is like thick darkness;
They do not know over what they stumble.

~ Proverbs 4:18

PHONING HER FRIEND, Ethel, Bessie bemoans recent parenting failures. She used poor judgment. She wasn't patient. Her tone was harsh. Thoughts of her failures undermine her confidence. What shall she do with failure?

Ethel reads Proverbs 4:18-19 and answers, "Spiritual growth is a process, not an arrival moment. We start life stumbling around in the moonless dark of sin. In salvation, light dawns. We see enough to start on the narrow way. As we study and obey the Word, the light brightens. The brighter the light, the more dirt we see to wipe off and the more we realize how dirty we were before.[1]

"There are still shadows, so we trip, fall into sin and get dirty, but the Word gives light to get up, wipe off the dirt, and walk on (Proverbs 24:16). The light rises higher and brighter until, as in full daylight, there are no shadows. As we behold the glory of the Lord (in the light of His Word) we 'are being transformed into the same image from glory to glory,' one godly thought or act to another (2 Corinthians 3:18).

"God uses failures to grow you in faith. Confess, believe in God's forgiveness, and move forward in obedience, trusting the Spirit for strength."

The next week Bessie complains, "I failed again!"

Ethel answers, "Yes, humans sin. God knows we are but dust. He forgives and restores with the compassion of a father (Psalm 103). Once you confess and repent, you can stop dwelling on yourself and turn your attention to our dear Lord Jesus and get busy serving Him."

That you aren't perfect probably isn't news to you. Yet, most parents intensely desire to parent right the first time, despite having little-to-no child-rearing experience. Sometimes you will feel angry or too tired to care, or too busy to notice. At one time or another, you will fail to meet a need, say the right words, feel only positive emotions, speak only gently in a way that gives grace, or discipline in the most godly and effective way.

If God has called you to repentance and faith in Christ, you have the

---

1. John Street, "Counseling and the Book of Proverbs," lecture series, The Master's University, 2010.

light of Christ in the Word of God. By reading and meditating on the Word, gaze at Jesus. Then do the next obedient thing. Being kind, all-wise, and all-powerful, God has the will and power to incorporate your failures—even sins—into His perfect plan for your growth and eventual perfection in a process called sanctification, ending in glorification.

"But the path of the righteous is like the light of dawn, that shines brighter and brighter until the fullness of day" (Psalm 4:18a).

Reflection

- If Bessie broods on her failures, how effective will she be at loving others? Why?
- Explain why, if we realize how corrupted by sin our hearts are, we would not be surprised by failures.
- How does the fact that spiritual growth is a process give you hope?

Implementation

- Is there a sin you have not confessed? Confess to God and, when it would not harm him, to the person against whom you sinned: "I did ____. It was wrong and sinful. Please forgive me."
- Consider a misjudgment or sin you have done in light of God's love.
  - Thank God for His mercies (name them).
  - Find what the Bible says to do instead.
  - Plan specific godly actions different from what you did before.
  - Do the next thing, trusting God's grace.
- Plan to counter morbid introspection. On a card list:
  - An emergency *thought* that will stop you in your tracks. ("Stop!" or, "Forgetting what lies behind …")
  - God-honoring *words* to tell yourself. ("There is no condemnation for those who are in Christ Jesus" [Romans 8:1].)
  - A God-honoring *action* you will do to move forward on the "path of the righteous."
  - On the back of the card, write a key verse that applies (Proverbs 4:18; 24:16; Philippians 3:13-14).
  - For one month, log your use of the instructions on this card and the difference it makes.

Feeling Shame? Look to Jesus

Therefore, since we have so great a cloud of witnesses surrounding us,
laying aside every weight and the sin which so easily entangles us,
let us run with endurance the race that is set before us,
fixing our eyes on Jesus, the author and perfecter of faith,
who for the joy set before Him endured the cross,
despising the shame, and has sat down at the right hand of
the throne of God. For consider Him who has endured
such hostility by sinners against Himself,
so that you will not grow weary, fainting in heart.

~ Hebrews 12:1-3

BESSIE OFTEN FEELS humiliated by the remorseless misconduct of her now-adult son, Donnie. Added to that is the weight of others' responses. One friend ostracized Bessie. Another hints that Bessie is to blame for Donnie's indigence. She was too strict or too permissive. Compensating for such deficient parents, Bessie's dad bought Donnie a cell phone. Some fault them for not supplying an apartment, insurance, and food. When Donnie was arrested, Bert felt shame on the family name.

Bessie realizes that she failed many times to parent biblically. She also repented, worked diligently to change, and parented well much more often than she failed. Yet Donnie scorns her. She feels disgraced.

Shame is an emotion common to parents of unbendingly wayward teens and adult children. Shame may be legitimate or illegitimate. Wrong-doing is rightly shameful, but being sinned against produces undeserved shame, such as what a rape victim feels.

There is also a shame of identity. Rather than, "You did a sinful action" (which can be forgiven), identity shame says, "You *are* a failure. You *are* a horrible parent." Or, though innocent of wrongdoing, by close connection you feel the shame of someone's disgraceful lifestyle.

Bessie needs the hope of Hebrews 12:1-3. It urges us to run the race of faith, discarding sins and unnecessary weights (like shame), keeping our eyes fixed on Jesus. He never sinned, yet others heaped shame upon Him. Family and friends abandoned Him. He was mocked, stripped, beaten, and hanged for public disgrace. Then, He took on the shame of sin that you and I deserve, by taking the guilt for sins and paying the price in our place. The cross was the most shameful experience in history.

How did He "despise the shame"? To "despise" means, "to think little of," to treat as insignificant. Jesus felt it, but was not controlled by it and did not let it dictate His identity or actions. In His view, undeserved shame was nothing compared to the joy ahead. Notice that joy counters shame.

No human parents live without both mistakes and sins. Confession and repentance removes the guilt. Any other sense of shame needs to be dealt with as Christ did. How? First, distinguish thoughts from feelings. What thought is producing the feeling? Then discern the truth based upon a scripture.

When you are falsely accused, don't try to defend yourself. It reinforces an accuser and puts you at risk of gossiping about your child. Ask yourself, "Is the accusation true?" If not, don't simmer that thought in your mental saucepan.

Refuse to listen to the shaming voices. Instead, talk to yourself. For example, do I feel vulnerable to ridicule? "I am clothed in the righteousness of Christ" (Philippians 3:9). Have I been rejected? "I am accepted in the Beloved" (Ephesians 1:6). Replace shame-inducing thoughts with right thoughts of Jesus, the author and perfecter of your faith. Meditate on His character and what He has done.

If you have loved your child in obedience to Scripture for the glory of God, you have obeyed God. He is your rewarder. Rejoice!

Reflection
- What is the difference between feelings and thoughts? How does each influence the other?
- What was ahead for Jesus that would be cause for joy? In Christ, what lies ahead of you that is cause for joy?

Implementation
- Consider Jesus: Read John 13-21. List what Jesus did while He approached and endured the shame of the cross. Thank and praise Him.
- List your shame-inducing thoughts. Then list Bible-based truths about God and yourself that directly counter them. Next time you feel shame, tell yourself these truths.
- If you tend to react angrily or become tongue-tied when falsely accused, consult a wise friend to plan right responses for the next time it happens. (Proverbs 26:4-5).

Die to Your Dream and Gain Heaven's Joy

*"If anyone comes to Me, and does not hate his own father and mother
and wife and children and brothers and sisters, yes, and even his own
life, he cannot be My disciple. Whoever does not carry his own cross
and come after Me cannot be My disciple."*

~ Luke 14:26-27

To CARRY A cross is to walk to your death, losing all you have on earth. Following Christ requires dying to anything and anyone you love more than you love God. Compared to your love for Jesus, all other loves should look like hate. This means we have to love Him more than we love anyone, even family.

This is a hard truth. Loving our children passionately, we can't stand to see them hurt, so we strive to keep them happy and get them spiritually saved. We want them to behave well. We long for reciprocal love. Most of all, we want them saved and their continued lostness is one of the most painful situations in parenting, a heavy burden, and a source of anguish.

These pursuits are good, but followed too intensely, they result in disobedience to Christ through over-protection, over-discipline, worry, and setting our happiness on having well-behaved, Christian children. We unwittingly become child-centered rather than Christ-centered. Our children become our idols.

Loving Jesus preeminently will cost you. It will mean giving up the dream of an ideal family. It will mean giving up peace in the home in order to hold the line on rules. It will certainly (and frequently) require making your child unhappy with you when you discipline him as the Bible commands; you will risk losing his love. It could mean one day removing your child from the home, lest he continues living off of you indefinitely. It certainly requires staking your happiness on the love of Christ, even if you don't have the love of your child. It will demand contentment with the will of God, even if your child is not saved.

Secondary goals (such as children who are saved and skilled in living) are helpful as long as they remain in subordination to God's primary purpose for you. Parents rightly hope for the salvation of their children and peace in the home, but if they want what God wants, they will trust Him with His will.

Parents can have some pretty rough days when children are being difficult. If we deny ourselves and obey Christ, we will have followed Christ. And if we follow Christ then we can rejoice even when family life does not go well.

The pursuit of His glory is so satisfying that it minimizes the pain we feel when our desires are not met. If all your parenting efforts fail and your child remains an unbeliever, yet you have parented first and foremost to please God, you can rejoice because you will have achieved God's most important goal.

Die to your dreams, live for God's will, and gain heaven's joy.

Reflection

- Do you ever sin in response to your child's disrespect or disobedience? What does that tell you about what you are most wanting at that moment?
- Do you experience anger, prolonged sadness, or despair over your child? How do those feelings affect your walk and relationship with Jesus Christ?
- What difference does it make when you give up your desires and follow Christ?

Implementation

- List goals you have for your children/family. Which ones would be most difficult to never have fulfilled?
- When your child persists in rejecting you and your home is not at peace, what do you need to change in order to rejoice in pleasing God?
- What God-honoring thought can you tell yourself when your child disappoints you? For example, "I don't need to have my daughter love me. What I need is to love the Lord."

*A Mother's
Joyful Enablement*

MEDITATION 32:

Hardship Is Opportunity

It was good for me that I was afflicted,
That I may learn Your statutes.

~ Psalm 119:71

IGNORANCE OFTEN RESULTS in negative consequences in health, prosperity, relationships, and loss of ability to enjoy blessings. Although learning can be difficult, the intent of childhood schooling is that information and skills gained enable the student to flourish in society over a lifetime.

According to Psalm 119:71, affliction is a form of schooling—a means to learn God's statutes, with the blessings they bestow. The world views affliction as punishment or a sign of shame or deserved disapproval. God intends it to benefit the afflicted.

The central profitable lesson of Psalm 119:71 is the learning of God's Word, learning that includes doing. Before affliction, the psalmist went his own way, but affliction drove him to God's Word and taught him obedience (119:67), the essential path to God's favor and abundant life in all ways. That is why the Word of God is "better to me than thousands of gold and silver pieces" (119:72). If affliction helps us on this path, then it is good, indeed!

My friend and fellow counselor says, "Adoption is good. Adoption is hard. Hard is not bad."[1] The discipline of hardship drives the believer to more fervently value the truth of the Word and the promises of God, so it offers opportunities.

We can clarify the right view *of God.*
- He is sovereign (even over evil), wise, good, and caring (Romans 8:28-29; 1 Peter 5:7).
- He turns evil to good, using circumstances for our welfare (Genesis 50:20; Colossians 1:24; 2 Corinthians 12:7-10; 1 Peter 1:6-7; Matthew 5:11-12; Ephesians 2:4-7).
- Who else do you want in charge of your suffering?

We can gain the right view *of self.*
- Everyone suffers (Job 5:7). Even when I suffer, I am not a victim, but a chooser (James 1:2-3).

---

1. Connie Dugas, at an Adoptive Moms' Meet, 2020.

We can practice God's answers to questions *on circumstances and trials.*
- In prayer, draw closer to God, who cares (1 Peter 5:7).
- Trust God, not self (Proverbs 3:5-6).
- See how God is faithful to enable right responses (1 Colossians 10:13).
- "Consider it all joy" for the growth you will gain by perseverance in trials. (James 1:2-3, 12).
- Respond God's way to conflict (Romans 12:9-21).
- Learn how to (1) not be overcome by evil, but (2) overcome evil with good (Romans 12:21).

Rightly handled, hardship helps us turn from sin and rebellion (Psalm 119:67). We learn to do our duty despite feelings to the contrary. We increase godly character (2 Corinthians 1:3-5). We reap joy (James 1:2-3).

In hardships we get to see what God will do with something beyond our control. If we obey Him we get to participate with God in His use of our circumstances for His glory and our good. The question to accomplish that purpose is, "What does the Word of God say I can do in my situation to glorify God, serve others, and grow in godliness?"

Reflection

🙢 Why do/should hardships drive a Christian to the Word of God?

🙢 Recall some hardships of your past. What Scripture verses provide guidance about them?

Implementation

🙢 Study the passages in this meditation and list what you learn about hardship. (Add these also: Romans 5:1-11; James 1:2-3, 12; 1 Peter 2:20-25; 4:19; Hebrews 12:4-11.)

🙢 Choose a word, phrase, or sentence in this meditation to be a key or trigger to move you to right thinking and responses.

🙢 Hardship drives us to seek answers to tough questions and those answers are in the Word of God, not in our experiences. In your next hardship, consider not "What does God want (by this experience) to teach me?" but, "What does Scripture say to do?":
  - How can I love and honor Jesus in my situation?
  - How can I love the person who sins against me?
  - How can I use my situation for eternal advantage for myself or others?

Be Strong

Finally, be strong in the Lord and in the strength of His might.

~ Ephesians 6:10

KNOWING THEY WOULD need it, Paul placed the above admonition at the end of his letter to the Ephesians. After giving them essential truths about God, themselves, their salvation, and their church (Ephesians 1-3), Paul called on them to walk worthy of their calling (ch. 4-6). It would require revolutionizing their lives. They were to think differently, renewing the mind. They were to act differently, replacing dishonesty, anger, filthy words, bitterness, immorality, and excessive desires with honesty, self-control, kindness, and forgiveness (ch. 4-5). They had to do all of this by the power of the Spirit in the nitty-gritty of relationships like family, living contentedly and intentionally in the roles of wife and husband, child and parent (ch. 5-6).

Such a transformation process is a spiritual war. To succeed, we must be strong, strong with God's strength, not our own. It is all possible only under the control and power of the Spirit. Godly living, especially amidst challenges and trials, is accomplished only through trusting the Lord to enable our obedience.

Godly parenting requires courage and strength, adoptive parenting even more so. Your precious adopted child's view of life and relationships may be complicated by experiences of loss, maltreatment, and other influences that shaped his attitudes and behaviors before he arrived at your door. Those will challenge you, perhaps in ways you never dreamed a child could do. You'll meet situations that require more wisdom and love than you have within yourself. The Lord has plenty and, by His Spirit, will give you the love you need.

Dealing with inner temptations will be hard enough. You'll also have temptations presented by the child, your family, and your community. You may experience confusion, unending challenges to your authority, and dashed parental hopes. You may be tempted to over-protectiveness, over-zealousness, passivity, anger, fear, or discouragement. You may have to persevere in discipline when all your feelings tell you to hug the child and let him go play. You may have to endure child services investigating your parenting. You may have to call the police to report a runaway. What will you do when your emotional response weakens your judgment?

You *must* be strong and fearless. Any sign of weakness or fear in a parent incites insecurity in a child. Children also see an opportunity to take advantage.

"Be strong in the Lord and in the strength of His might." Keep yourself seeking God's counsel in the Word of God—daily and for problems that arise. Then, keep depending upon Him to enable obedience regardless of your feelings.

Reflection

- What feelings tend to drain your strength of character or your courage?
- When you feel drained, where do you turn for strength? Where does the Bible say to turn?
- What challenges in parenting have most stressed or stretched you?
- How does Ephesians 6:10 relate to the commands in 6:4 to model godliness ("do not provoke"), instruct, and discipline?

Implementation

- Identify a weakness in your parenting. What Bible verse speaks to this? Pray and plan how to apply the verse in your next parenting action.
- Be strong in the Word. List what Proverbs says about these categories: children, speech, anger, and honesty. Be strong in praying these verses.
- Be the parent. Rate yourself (1-10) on the following.
  - hugging and praising your children many times per day ___
  - decision-making (not looking to the children for guidance) ___
  - instructing clearly ___
  - holding firm to enforce when you say no ___
  - speaking kindly and gently when tempted to be angry ___
  - living joyfully when life seems to fall apart ___
- If you spot a weak area, prayerfully and specifically take action. Ask your spouse or a spiritual friend to advise and periodically ask for a report.

Parent Fearlessly

Yahweh is my light and my salvation;
Whom shall I fear?
Yahweh is the strong defense of my life;
Whom shall I dread?

~ Psalm 27:1

DAVID WROTE THE above passage when an entire army was threatening him (27:2-3). How could he refuse to fear? He began with a right view of God—"my salvation." A few insights from the whole psalm include:

- He saw the reality—God is salvation more powerful than any army (vss. 1-3).
- He counseled his own heart to not fear but be confident (vs. 3).
- He loved God more than safety (vs. 4).
- He chose joy in relationship with God, not anxiety (vs. 6).
- He practiced obedience despite provocation otherwise (vss. 11-12).
- He willfully chose to trust God and take courage (vss. 13-14).

A child craving control will do everything he can to wrench control from parents, endlessly undermining parental authority. An adoptive mom can grow fearful. Fear that discipline will damage her child provokes a lack of confidence and inconsistent discipline. Sensing her hesitation, the child takes advantage. Rebellion and manipulations can confuse thought and undermine confidence. Aggression intimidates. Fear of investigation and of losing children to child protective services hinders her from calling the police when she should. Fatigue and despair exacerbate it all.

Trusting God, Mom must be fearless, bold, and confident. This is true with all children, but especially the rebellious. As the running of prey automatically triggers a predator to chase and overpower, any show of weakness or fear in a mother is like gasoline poured on a rebel's boldness. It also chills the trust of the siblings who wonder, "Is she in control? Can she protect me?"

Mothers must never show fear of a child, not even when physically endangered. As one mom told her son, "You need to know that if you kill me, I will gain everything good and you will not. I gain Jesus and heaven and a perfected body. You will have only pain. God has already decided when and how I will die and you can't override His will" (paraphrased).[1]

---

1. D.S., of Georgia, identity protected, interviewed by me, November 2021.

How can a mother be fearless in parenting? Psalm 27 is one source of counsel.

- Practice right thinking about God. God is my omnipotent salvation, more powerful than anyone. Fear Him and no other (vss. 1-3).
- Seek to love God much more than your safety and comfort. Be willing to lose all. Be satisfied with Christ even in loss. Love overcomes fear (vs. 4).
- Believe God can bring good out of any evil (love thinks well of the other) (vss. 5-6; 1 Corinthians 13:7).
- Rejoice in God and sing. Joy drives away fear (vs. 6; Ezekiel 7:7).
- Refuse to worry. Pray, think right, do right (vs. 6; Philippians 4:6-9).
- Parent obediently regardless of the child's response or your losses (vss. 11-12).
- Willfully choose to trust God and take courage. Tell your heart to "be strong and let your heart take courage" (vss. 12-14).

Reflection

- In what ways have you noticed a lack of parental confidence in yourself or others?
- Why is fearlessness so important in child-rearing? (There are more reasons than those listed above.)
- Love and joy are incompatible with fear (Psalm 27:4, 6; Ezekiel 7:7; 1 John 4:18). How can this truth be applied?
- How does doubting God relate to fear?

Implementation

- Study Psalm 27.
  - List the principles. There are more than were listed in this meditation.
  - Plan how and when to implement one of the principles.
    - in your mind,
    - in your face and body language,
    - in how you speak (for example, with authority as well as respect),
    - in what you do.
  - Memorize a key verse from Psalm 27 and pray it morning, evening, and any time you lack confidence.
  - Over the next month, log your application of Psalm 27 concerning fearlessness.
- Study these verses and apply them as above: Matthew 14:25-31; Luke 12:4-5; Proverbs 16:6; Psalm 56:4; 91:5-6; 112:1, 4, 7-8; Proverbs 29:25; 1 John 4:17-18.

Seek to Bless Your Wayward Child

"… love your enemies, do good to those who hate you, bless those who curse you, pray for those who disparage you."

~ Luke 6:27-28

DONNIE HAS CEASELESSLY defied, demeaned, and shamed Bessie for years. Now out of the home, he still stirs trouble. He calls with fake apologies and asks for money, then texts cutting accusations. Portraying himself as a victim, he turns others against his parents. He behaves like an enemy. Bert and Bessie are heartbroken and tempted toward resentment. Bessie wants to distance herself emotionally, scold him, block his number, and tell others what he is really like underneath the charm.

Jesus said, "… love your enemies, do good to those who hate you, bless those who curse you, pray for those who disparage you." Think of how Jesus carried out this command on the cross. He gave up His life for His enemies (Romans 5:6, 8, 10). While dying, He prayed that the Father would forgive them.

Feeling hurt and disappointed, parents can grow resentful, unforgiving, and cynical. They need to think in light of God's glory and purposes. Relational problems are not primarily about Mom and her pain. The child's war is against God. He is not your enemy; he is a mission field. Seek to win him to the Lord.

Regarding offenses, Romans 12 says, "Never paying back evil for evil … never taking your own revenge … Do not be overcome by evil" (12:17, 21). You may grieve your child's sin and your losses, but you must not sin.

Verse 21 also tells what to do instead, "overcome evil with good." Find ways to "do good to [one] who hates you." For example, "if your enemy is hungry, feed him." Note that food is an essential, not an extra. Meeting needs must be done wisely. Moms tend to overdo and actually enable continued irresponsibility and sinful behaviors. It is not loving to give money indiscriminately to a drug addict or to pay gambling debts. Lack of negative consequences prolong a refusal to repent. His repentance to believe the gospel is the greatest good.

Overcoming with good requires effort, so Romans 12:17 says "respecting [planning and providing for] what is good." Plan good and provide how you'll do it. Plan how you will manage conversations; "so far as it depends on you, being at peace with all men" (12:18). In other words, do what you can to not unnecessarily offend and to promote peace without enabling sin.

"Bless those who curse you." Blessing is God-like. The first thing God did after creation was to bless it. The theme of blessing can be traced from Genesis 1 to the very last chapter. God delights to bless. We should too.

Blessing does not mean always saying "Yes." It may mean speaking a truth he doesn't want to hear, but in a gentle way with encouragement. It may require refusing a request if helping him would enable continued sin and prevent consequences he needs for learning wisdom. Love dictates.

Speak well of the child to others. Defending yourself from accusations draws attention to you, not to the problem or the Lord. The words with which you answer must be God-honoring truth, spoken in love with gentleness intended for the welfare of the other.

Pray for your child. Continue to love your wayward child wisely. Seek to bless.

Reflection

- What do Luke 6:27 and Romans 12:9-21 teach about how to treat someone who acts like an enemy?
- How do the two summary commands in verse 21 relate to fulfilling the whole passage?
- What is the difference between blessing your child and giving him what he wants?
- How enthusiastic are you about seeking to bless your child? How might these passages help?

Implementation

- Plan thoughts and actions to turn from anger and practice love.
- List some specific prayers you might pray for your child. (Possible verses include: Proverbs 1:7; 9:10; 10:1; 13:10; 19:23; Matthew 22:37, 39; Luke 9:23; James 4:6, 7, 10; 2 Corinthians 5:9, 14-15)
- Ask your spouse, a wise friend, or your pastor for ways you might wisely overcome evil with good. For six months, record what you do. How does it help lessen resentment and increase your desire to bless?
- Are you confident that your child knows he could come and find you respectfully receptive to reconciliation?

Draw Near for Grace

For we do not have a high priest who cannot sympathize with our weaknesses, but One who has been tempted in all things like we are, yet without sin. Therefore let us draw near with confidence to the throne of grace, so that we may receive mercy and find grace to help in time of need.

~ Hebrews 4:15-16

THE CHRISTIAN HAS a great high priest mediating for us to the Holy One. Jesus, the Son of God, paid full atonement and accomplished complete redemption. The sacrifice for the sins of a Christian need never again be made.

This priest is neither elite nor untouchable. Although Jesus could not sin, He was able to experience temptation. His temptation was greater than ours could ever be because He never gave in, while we give in when the pressure gets heavy enough. Because He endured life on earth as a human, He knows what it is like to live here and suffer from sin's effects. He understands. For us, that means we can draw near to Him with confidence that we may receive mercy and find grace to help in times of need. Grace is enablement to obey. He will be kind and give us what will enable us to resist temptations and walk godly in our trials.

How does this relate to parents? The self-denial required for parenting is hard enough. Add the demand of dealing with sin from everyone in the family. Compound it with the adopted child's reactions to trauma and loss. Naturally, parents face many temptations.

Like anyone, they are tempted to indulge their desires. When tired, they want to rest, not get up to deal with a disciplinary situation. When hungry, they want to eat, not wait on a child with coordination problems. At misbehavior, they may be provoked into anger. They are tempted to tire of giving and giving to a child who is never satisfied, of taking precautions with a child who can never be trusted.

Parents with alienated, oppositional children are constantly tested with manipulations, lies, thefts, inconsistent affection, and antagonism, tempted with worry, loneliness, self-pity, and grief. It is hard to graciously endure continued rejection, to love in the face of accusations, to answer manipulations wisely and gently. Grieving parents are tempted to despair and cynicism.

In all cases, we have a great high priest who can sympathize with our weaknesses because He has been tempted in all things like we are, yet without sin. He gave and gave, and still, people wanted more from Him. He gave and gave, and still, people wanted more from Him. Those He loved were stubborn and insubordinate. Like alienated children do, they whined, walked away, challenged with antagonistic questions, and picked verbal fights with Him. They mocked, reviled, and accused Him of doing wrong. He felt extreme grief at the loss of relationship with them in their obstinate rejection. Jesus kept sacrificing His needs and desires and even giving His life for them while they accused Him of not loving them.

Therefore let us draw near with confidence to the throne of grace, so that we may receive mercy and find grace to help in time of need.

- Draw near for mercy. Not yet perfected, you will sin and need daily fatherly forgiveness and cleansing from sins so that you can continue forward with a clear conscience.
- Draw near for grace. We need enablement to resist sin and obey God.

Reflection

- What temptations do you think dealing with people came to Jesus? How is that comforting to you?
- What has Christ done for you? How does that motivate you to respond to Him?
- How does God's mercy to you influence your perspective when your child sins?

Implementation

- What sin is tempting you today? Or what parenting command do you find difficult to obey today? What are two actions you can take to draw near to the throne for grace to obey? Do them, and later tell a trusted confidant how God's grace enabled you.
- The next time your child sins, remind yourself of the sympathy Jesus has for you. Record how this truth influenced your attitude and demeanor toward your child.

The Joy of the Lord Is Your Strength

Then he said to them, "Go, eat of the fat, drink of the sweet, and send portions to him who has nothing prepared; for this day is holy to our Lord. Do not be grieved, for the joy of Yahweh is your strength."

~ Nehemiah 8:10

PERHAPS YOU'VE HAD an especially difficult season in parenting. Or perhaps it seems like the pressures of parenting will never end. Or maybe your trial is something altogether different. Whatever the case, you feel disheartened, robbed of joy, and drained of energy. Consider these questions and their inferences:

- Is God sovereign? Yes, so you know your present situation is God's will for you for now.
- Is God good? Yes, so you know He has a good intent for the situation.
- Does God love you? Yes, so all that is happening is in some way best for you.

Knowing these things, you must trust Him. It will demonstrate your love for Him.

Here is another guiding truth. "The joy of the Lord is your strength." How? What does joy have to do with the strength to endure difficulties in a God-honoring way?

Consider Ezekiel 7:7. Under judgment, some Israelites had been deported to Babylon. The prophet Ezekiel was one of them. From there, he prophesied that final judgment was coming. He said, "Your doom has come to you, O inhabitant of the land. The time has come, the day is near—*tumult rather than joyful shouting* on the mountains" (Ezekiel 7:7, emphasis mine). Ezekiel had a point for this verse, but as a side note, notice that terror and despair are juxtaposed with joy. Apparently, despair and joy are mutually exclusive. In other words, joy has the power to drive out dread and despair.

Later, in Nehemiah's day, some Israelites returned to the desolated land. Nehemiah 8 records that when Ezra the scribe read the law to them, they realized that their awful punishment in Babylon was for violating that law. They mourned. However, what Ezra read revealed also that God is gracious; He had not completely destroyed them but brought some back to the land. It was a day to worshipfully celebrate, "Go, eat of the fat, drink of the sweet . . . Do not be grieved, for the joy of Yahweh is your strength." Joy would give them strength to overcome their despair and face trials in the coming days. Joy in Yahweh drives out despair and infuses strength.

In hardships, we usually don't feel like rejoicing. Encouragement to do so sounds unreasonable, even harsh, maybe impossible! Actually, joy is a solution, not just a result of improved circumstances.

From jail, Paul commanded the suffering Philippians, "Rejoice!" (Philippians 4:4). James told suffering Christians, "Consider it all joy, my brothers, when you encounter various trials" (James 1:2). We *can* choose joy.

Joy in Christ is not only the end we hope for; it is the means to that end. We don't obey God, hoping for happy feelings. In the midst of the trial, we choose to rejoice in Christ and when we do, we find that the act of rejoicing gives us strength to endure in a God-glorifying manner that produces more joy. It works like food to a starving prisoner, like glucose tablets to a marathoner. Joy strengthens.

What a marvelous solution to fear or despair! God wants His children to experience joy.

Reflection

- Why does rejoicing give strength to live godly in trials?
- How can you rejoice when discouragement has robbed you of energy and desire?

Implementation

- Here are a few ideas for how to practice rejoicing. Choose one and do it. Later, choose another.
  - Read and pray through Psalms such as 27, 33, 93, 99, 103, 104, 131, 135, 139, or 148.
  - Sing hymns and spiritual songs.
  - Skim through a Bible book and rehearse the mighty works God has done. Thank Him.
  - Call or visit a friend and tell her insights you've gained from praising God with His psalms.
- Create a list of reasons to rejoice. Add to the suggestions below:
  - Having a loving Father
  - Union with Christ
  - The Holy Spirit indwelling and working His will
  - Christ indwelling, the hope of glory
  - Being a citizen of heaven
  - Being a member of the body of Christ

Resources

Psalms Especially Helpful

The psalms cover the extensive range of human experiences and emotions and connect them to relationship with God. They teach doctrine applied. A psalm can lead you in lament or swell your heart with joy. Praying through a psalm can readjust your perspective, comfort, bolster courage, and reinforce fortitude. Most importantly, it is a rich means of worship and fellowship with God the Father and the Savior Jesus Christ. The psalms listed below address various issues, from solitude to conflict, despair to joy. Find one that fits your present situation and let it shape your heart and lead you in worship of our God who is almighty and gentle, just and merciful, perfectly right and abundantly compassionate.

PSALMS 13, 27, 31, 37, 42, 46, 51, 55, 73, 112, 139, 145

Print Resources

LINDA J. RICE:
>   *Parenting the Difficult Child: A Biblical Perspective on Reactive Attachment Disorder*

AMY BAKER, EDITOR:
>   *Caring for the Souls of Children: A Biblical Counselor's Manual*

JERRY BRIDGES:
>   *Trusting God Even When Life Hurts*

LOU PRIOLO:
>   *Fear: Breaking Its Grip*
>   *Manipulation: Knowing How to Respond*

STUART SCOTT:
>   *Anger, Anxiety, and Fear: A Biblical Perspective*
>   *Communication and Conflict Resolution: A Biblical Perspective*
>   *From Pride to Humility: A Biblical Perspective*

MARTHA PEACE AND STUART W. SCOTT:
>   *The Faithful Parent: A Biblical Guide to Raising a Family*

JIM NEWHEISER AND ELYSE FITZPATRICK:
>   *You Never Stop Being a Parent*

DAVE HARVEY AND PAUL GILBERT:
>   *Letting Go: Rugged Love for Wayward Souls*

Online Resources

Linda J. Rice:

SeedSown, at https://seedsownpress.wordpress.com/category/
reactive-attachment-disorder/. See blog posts in the categories of
parenting and, especially, reactive attachment disorder.

Edward Lawrence:

Parents' Groans over Their Ungodly Children.
(2603 West Wright Street, Pensacola, Florida 32505 USA
Chapel Library: http://www.ChapelLibrary.org)
Phone: (850) 438-6666, Fax: (850) 438-0227.
Free download, 45 pages. (Consider sending Chapel Library a
donation.)

Association of Certified Biblical Counselors store:

Search for lectures on adoption and adoptive children and parents.
Also, Amy Baker on reactive attachment disorder.
See especially five break-out lectures on adoption issues from
the 2022 Annual Conference https://biblicalcounseling.com/
product/2022-in-his-image/ .

Counseling Resources

Your church leader

(Ephesians 4:11-16; Galatians 6:1-5; Romans 15:4, 14)

A wise woman in your church

(Titus 2:3-5)

Association of Certified Biblical Counselors "Find a Counselor":

https://biblicalcounseling.com/find-a-counselor/